From Touching Rock Bottom to Touching the Nations

How God Used a Teenage Alcoholic to Plant Ireland's Multicultural Church

By Nick Park

SSI

Success Services Ireland

From Touching Rock Bottom to Touching the Nations
Copyright © 2011 Nick Park
ISBN 978-0-9570750-0-9

Printed in Ireland by SPRINT-print Ltd

Cover design by Kirsty Park

Photographs from Spit Records and Kirsty Park

Published by Success Services Ireland
Whitethorn House, Ballymakenny Road
Drogheda, County Louth
Ireland
www.nickpark.ie

ABOUT THE AUTHOR

Nick Park was raised in Belfast, Northern Ireland, and was won to Christ through the ministry of the Salvation Army. After graduation and ordination from the William Booth Memorial Training College in London, he and his wife, Janice, served as Salvation Army Officers in Leicester, and then in pastoral ministry with the Assemblies of God in Lancashire.

In 1994 they started the Solid Rock Church - known as 'Ireland's Multicultural Church.' They also founded the ministry of the Church of God in Ireland. Nick still serves as Senior Pastor of the Solid Rock Church, while Janice serves as Worship and Prayer Pastor.

Nick is Administrative Bishop of the Church of God in Ireland and Executive Director of Evangelical Alliance Ireland. He holds an MTh in Applied Theology from the University of Liverpool, and is Adjunct Professor in Church Growth at the Eurasian Theological Seminary in Moscow, Russia. He has been twice elected to the International Executive Council of the Church of God.

Nick and Janice Park have a daughter, Kirsty, and live in Dromin village in County Louth.

CONTENTS

INTRODUCTION

For me, it happened one Sunday morning in August 2001 in an over-crowded hotel ballroom in Drogheda, Ireland. The congregation's clothes were damp from the unseasonable shower of rain that had drenched them as they ran into the building for cover. My own jacket reeked of fried bacon and cigarette smoke – caused by the gauntlet we had to run every Sunday. The hotel's coffee lounge, through which we all had to pass to reach the function room, was a favourite spot for locals to grab a late Sunday morning breakfast and then chain smoke as they discussed the doings of the week. All in all, it seemed like the last place in the world where a Pastor would understand the very reason for his existence.

There are times in every Christian leader's life when you have to do stuff – good stuff, ministry stuff - that you know isn't what you really want to do. In fact, you know that it isn't really God's ultimate plan for your life either – but you do it anyway. You do it for a variety of reasons. You do it because nobody else is willing to do it. You do it because it's a part of your job or ministry position. You do it on the noble grounds that you have a servant heart and delight in helping others. Or maybe you do it on the less noble grounds that you want to keep everyone happy, and sometimes it's easier to just do the stuff you don't particularly enjoy than it is to deal with the hassle of unhappy Church people.

But, for the most part, you do stuff as a Christian leader because you believe that it *is* God's will for you to do so. You accept that this is just the way it works – that sometimes you have to do stuff that you don't particularly enjoy, in order to prepare you, and get you ready for God's ultimate plan for your life. And that is what ultimately keeps people going in Christian ministry – the belief that God has something planned and prepared for you that constitutes your real purpose in life. We all need to feel that we're going somewhere, not just running endlessly round on a treadmill.

It is this search for purpose that enables so many pastors and leaders to keep on going in the face of so many heartaches and disappointments. We recognise that much of what we go through is a preparation for God's ultimate plan for our lives. Therefore we can put up with all kinds of setbacks because we believe our path is taking us to the point where we can say, "Yes! This is the reason why God put me on the face of the planet. This is my destiny!"

Moses discovered this at the burning bush (Exodus 3:1-10). He was aware that God had a purpose for his life. His parents had shielded him from death because they knew he was no ordinary child. His adoptive parents had raised him with the entitlements and expectations of a Prince of Egypt. But until he knew exactly what it was he was supposed to do, he was in the same position as many of us who say we'll do 'anything for Jesus.' The problem was that a willingness to do an undefined *anything* is very different from knowing the specific *something* that God has prepared for us. Moses killed an abusive Egyptian overseer because he was willing to do anything, but it wasn't until his encounter with God at the burning bush that he understood that his calling was to bring the Israelites out of Egypt. From that moment forward Moses was focused. He knew why he existed.

That Sunday in August in Drogheda was a bit special. We were dedicating a few babies that morning. In fact it was more than a few – we were dedicating twenty-seven babies that morning! Over the last eight months God had transformed our congregation. An influx of immigration into Ireland, and the establishment of an asylum seeker centre a few miles outside Drogheda, had dramatically changed our numbers and ethnicity. It had been eight years since my wife and I had planted the Solid Rock Church. We had slowly grown to about seventy people, all of whom were white and Irish, worshipping on a Sunday morning. But suddenly, in just eight months, we had grown to over two hundred worshippers, evenly mixed between white Irish and black Africans. While we rejoiced in this growth, we were struggling to cope with new pastoral challenges and, perhaps more crucially, we were asking ourselves what God was really doing in all this process.

Because of an anomaly in the Irish Constitution, many of the asylum seekers coming to Ireland at that time were pregnant women from Africa, unaccompanied by their husbands. We discovered that offering to dedicate their new babies to God was a very fruitful form of outreach and evangelism. So that was why, on that particular Sunday morning, I found myself in the unprecedented position of dedicating twenty-seven babies in one service.

As the worship team began to really get into their stride, I was on the front row with my hands held high and joining in the praises to God. Then some movement to my right caught my eye. A young Nigerian mother needed to go to the toilets. She was on her own, so she did the most natural thing. She turned to the person standing next to her, asked "Will you hold my baby till I come back?" and made her way down the aisle towards the exit.

The person now holding the baby was Pat O'Boyle. Pat and his wife, Marcella, were much loved and respected in our church. Pat had retired, which made him a little unusual in that most of our church were much younger. He was also unusual in that he had served for many years as the Superintendent of Police in Drogheda. At that time Pentecostals were still viewed with suspicion and disfavour by many people, particularly those in the establishment. It was not uncommon for Catholic priests to publicly deride us as a cult. So it was rare for somebody like Pat O'Boyle, a respected pillar in the local community, to be so visibly involved with a Church like the Solid Rock.

I watched Pat as he continued to worship God, holding that little Nigerian/Irish baby in his arms. An old saying declares that 'A picture is worth a thousand words.' And if I had taken a photograph at the time then this book could have been a thousand words shorter! I was no longer singing along with the worship team, but at that moment I entered into a place of understanding and fellowship with God that is surely the goal of all true worship.

I tried to imagine where else in Ireland such a scene could ever occur. Where else would a pillar of the community like Pat O'Boyle stand side-by-side with a young asylum seeker from Nigeria? Where else would that young women feel so at ease as to hand her baby over to someone who was so different to her in just about every circumstance imaginable? Where else could I see such a scene, not as a staged photo opportunity, but as a natural expression of Ireland's future? Today, if I close my eyes, I can still see that scene preserved in every detail. It is as if God has burned that picture of Pat and the baby indelibly into my brain.

And that was the moment when it happened. That was the moment when I understood my destiny. That was the point when I realised that this was why God had put me on the face of planet earth. This was no longer God preparing me for some great thing in the future – this was the great thing, and it wasn't just in the future anymore.

I understood that the changes we had been seeing in the Solid Rock Church, and the image of Pat O'Boyle holding that baby, were a picture of what was to come. In a world that is cruelly divided, and living in a nation that has suffered so much from religious and political division, I was to dedicate my life and ministry to breaking down the walls that separate believers from each other. As the New Testament puts it, Christ has destroyed the barrier, or the dividing wall of hostility, so as to create in Himself one new humanity (Ephesians 2:14-15).

One of the key axioms of the Church Growth Movement is the power of the Homogeneous Unit Principle. Quite simply, this can be summed up in the old proverb that says 'Birds of a feather flock together.' It has been demonstrated that Churches start easier and grow faster when we reach out to people who are most like us. This is why immigrant Churches multiply so effectively. In a strange and alien society people tend to gather with their compatriots – which is why in North America and Europe we see so many African Churches, Indian Churches, Filipino Churches, Brazilian Churches, Korean Churches etc.

But, and this is a huge *but*, the same force that makes evangelism among immigrants easy also makes true discipleship difficult. It's not that the Homogeneous Unit Principle is good or bad – it's more like a law of nature that just *is*. Gravity, for example, is neither good nor bad. Gravity can work for you, or it can work against you. When you sit down on a chair, then gravity makes that process easier. If you don't believe me, then just watch footage of astronauts in the International Space Station trying to pull themselves into a chair in a weightless environment. They have to work hard to prevent themselves from floating away from the chair! Yet gravity can work against you – for example, if you slip when you are standing on a high ladder!

In the same way, Church leaders need to learn both how to make the Homogeneous Unit Principle work for them in evangelism and yet to overcome the same principle when it works against them in creating disciples. It is no good establishing new Churches if those same Churches serve to isolate us and separate us from Christians who look, talk and act differently from ourselves.

That Sunday morning I caught hold of God's purpose for my life – to blaze a trail for Christians from different backgrounds and nationalities to worship and grow in grace together. That is a huge calling for any Christian leader to try to get their head around. For me it was particularly daunting given my past history as a homeless alcoholic who used to sleep on the sectarian-riven streets of Belfast, Northern Ireland. God's plan was to take a man who had touched rock bottom and then use him to touch the nations.

1

THE EMPTINESS WITHIN

"Are you stupid? She's dead!"

With those words the life of a very young child was altered forever. I was only three years old, but I somehow realised that everything had been irrevocably changed. From this moment onwards no-one could be depended upon, and nothing could be trusted. Most of all I understood that loving someone opens a door to experiencing a very special kind of pain and loss – a pain and loss that nobody was ever going to impose on me ever again.

Our family was living in a suburb of East Belfast. Although I had been born in Wythenshawe in the North of England, my father, David Park, had come to Ireland to lecture in microbiology at Queen's University in Belfast. In the winter of 1965 my mother, Maurine, fell ill with colitis. Trying to work at the University and also care for a sick wife and four young boys aged from eight months to six years was obviously an impossible task for any man. So I ended up staying with my grandmother in Yorkshire for a while.

My mother died on Christmas Day 1965. My grandmother told me many years later that a hospital doctor known for his cynicism, observing how my father cared for my mother, remarked that his faith in marriage had been restored. But, as I said, that was many years later. At the time my grandmother told me nothing. I was left blissfully unaware of my motherless status.

I've often wondered why she didn't tell me. Was it a conversation that was simply too hard to initiate? Did she think I was too young to understand death? Some years later I asked my grandmother why. She simply replied, "It wasn't my job."

A bad case of the whooping cough delayed my return to Belfast. Eventually, when I finally returned home, I was like any three year old child who hadn't seen his mother for weeks. I jumped out of the car and ran into the house. My two elder brothers, Stephen and John, were playing at the foot of the staircase. I couldn't wait! I yelled at the top of my voice, "I'm home! Where's mum?" They stared at me.

I was only three years old, but I remember that moment so vividly. Over the ensuing years I would dream it again and again – and every time it was the same. A silence that seemed to last for ever. Two pairs of eyes staring at me. A growing awareness that somehow, without knowing how or why, I had said something wrong and put my foot in it. Then I heard those words, "Are you stupid? She's dead!"

My brothers were only aged five and six. I don't even know which of them it was who spoke. To them, no doubt, it was a simple child-like response to a kid brother who didn't seem to know something that the whole world seemed to know. But to me it felt as if my world had just dropped away from beneath my feet. I knew that I was feeling a pain such as I had never dreamed existed, and I knew that the pain was so great because I had loved my mother so much. Even at three years old I understood that there was only one way to make sure that no-one would ever hurt me that much again. "I'm never going to love anyone again," I murmured. Children say all kinds of things they don't mean. But my tragedy was that for the next fifteen years I would keep the promise I made to myself that day.

Growing up without loving anyone isn't actually that hard to do. Children are naturally self-centred anyway. I quickly learned what benefited me and what didn't. I did what made me feel good. I have no doubt that my father loved me, and, after he remarried, I know that my step-mother loved me also. But I can't ever remember feeling any love for them in return. I learned how to smile back and respond in an appropriate way. I learned how to turn on the charm when I needed to talk my way out of trouble. But inside there was nothing but a big black hole where my affections should be.

Recently I came across an article by Dr Michael Conner, a psychologist. He writes:

"A psychopath is usually a subtle manipulator. They do this by playing to the emotions of others. They typically have high verbal intelligence, but they lack what is commonly referred to as 'emotional intelligence'. There is always a shallow quality to the emotional aspect of their stories. In particular they have difficulty describing how they felt, why they felt that way, or how others may feel and why. In many cases you almost have to explain it to them. Close friends and parents will often end up explaining to the psychopath how they feel and how others feel who have been hurt by him or her. They can do this over and over with no significant change in the person's choices and behaviour. They don't understand or appreciate the impact that their behaviour has on others. They do appreciate what it means when they are caught breaking rules or the law even though they seem to end up in trouble again. They desperately avoid incarceration and loss of freedom but continue to act as if they can get away with breaking the

rules. They don't learn from these consequences. They seem to react with feelings and regret when they are caught. But their regret is not so much for other people as it is for the consequences that their behaviour has had on them, their freedom, their resources and their so called 'friends.' They can be very sad for their self. A psychopath is always in it for their self even when it seems like they are caring for and helping others. The definition of their 'friends' are people who support the psychopath and protect them from the consequence of their own antisocial behaviour. Shallow friendships, low emotional intelligence, using people, antisocial attitudes and failure to learn from the repeated consequences of their choices and actions help identify the psychopath."

When I first read that, my blood ran cold. I thought to myself, "This guy is describing my childhood and adolescence more accurately than people who have known me all my life!" From three years old and onwards, my feelings and actions towards family, teachers or indeed anyone else, were indistinguishable from those of a psychopath.

I certainly didn't have a deprived childhood, not by any stretch of the imagination. We lived in an upper middle class area. We were well fed and well clothed. Every year we took two holidays – two weeks with relatives in England during the Easter school holidays, and three weeks in a self-catering chalet in Donegal during the Summer holidays. All of the Park children, myself included, were of above average intelligence and passed the necessary examinations to attend Grammar School. If affluence and education were all that was necessary for happiness then I should have been the happiest child in Ireland. As it was, I was miserable, empty, and continually felt that I was an outsider who didn't belong.

Sometimes I felt like running away from home. Running *from* was no problem – but where could I run *to*? I was aware that I didn't belong at home, but neither did I belong anywhere else. After all, growing up in Northern Ireland during the late 1960's and early 1970's, the world outside was a pretty scary place.

The sectarian violence, popularly known as 'The Troubles,' had really kicked off in earnest in 1969. For the next twenty-five years the newspapers would report a daily litany of riots, explosions and shootings. Each atrocity seemed to plumb new depths of hate and barbarism. In January 1972 British Paratroopers opened fire on unarmed Catholic civil rights protesters, killing fourteen in what came to be known as 'Bloody Sunday'. In July of that same year the IRA detonated twenty-two bombs in one night, killing nine victims in bars and commercial premises across Belfast. In fact, in that one year, the IRA carried out over thirteen hundred bombings, killing over a hundred British soldiers and injuring five hundred more. Night after night I could hear the bombs exploding as I lay in my bed. Loyalist paramilitaries, drawn from the Protestant community, were no less bloodthirsty. The Shankill Butchers were a gang that would kidnap Catholics at random from the street, torture them brutally, and then cut their throats or chop them to death with a hatchet.

But behind the headline atrocities there were thousands of lesser acts of violence that went unreported. I quickly learned that, when out and about in Belfast, you had always to be alert as to where you were. For a Protestant to be caught in a Catholic area, or vice-versa, could result in a fearsome beating. As a matter of survival you learned to read your surroundings. Graffiti on walls was one indication. Political slogans or the names of football teams told you if you were among your own, or if you were on enemy turf. If school buildings or community centres were named after a saint then you were in a Catholic district. You scanned the names of shops to see if the proprietors were Catholic or Protestant. Even by-passers' accents carried subtle clues in the way certain words were pronounced.

Foreigners were often mystified by this conflict. Why on earth would Christians fight each other over religion? The truth, of course, was that the conflict was tribal, not theological. Centuries ago English monarchs encouraged Scottish Presbyterian settlers to migrate into the north-eastern corner of Ireland, grabbing land and displacing native Irish farmers. 'Protestant' and 'Catholic' have become useful, but often misleading, shorthand to refer to the Scots-Irish and to the descendants of the native Irish. So, in Northern Ireland, 'Protestant' and 'Catholic' are tribal designations that refer to an accident of birth. Even if you are an atheist then you will either be a Protestant atheist or a Catholic atheist!

For the children of the Park family, growing up in Belfast was made even more complicated by the fact that we were among the few people who didn't belong to either tribe.

My parents had moved from England to Northern Ireland in the 1960's, and as such they had no history of, and no interest in, the sectarian tribalism. Northern Irish politics are based on long memories, bearing grudges for events that happened three hundred years ago, so it is well-nigh impossible for recent immigrants to understand or adopt the depths of bitterness involved. Also, we lived in an upper middle class suburb that had not been subjected to the ethnic cleansing that had characterised the more impoverished inner city.

In 1969 and 1970 the working class areas of Belfast and other Northern Irish towns and cities had seen families burned out of their homes in systematic campaigns to produce ghettos that belonged exclusively to one tribe. In some cases a 'Peace Line' (a huge concrete wall or steel fence) had to be erected to keep the warring factions apart. But for the middle classes, things were less segregated. Catholic dentists or lawyers lived side by side with Protestant academics or civil servants. To be sure, some sectarian attitudes still persisted among the middle classes, but not to anything like the degree that prevailed in the ghettos of the Falls Road or the Shankill Road.

But, for our family, there was one more component that ensured we could never belong to one tribe or the other – my father was a Quaker. Quakers were a small minority in Ireland, but they were famous for their stance on non-violence, and their commitment to peace meant they attempted to treat both communities in Northern Ireland impartially. When the British government had introduced internment (basically imprisonment without trial or evidence for anyone suspected of terrorism) the Quakers responded by running a minibus service that freely carried the relatives of both Republican and Loyalist internees to visit their men 'behind the wire.' Quakers quickly became perceived as something different, neither Catholic nor Protestant.

The problem with ghettos is that they are formed to exclude the outsider. Growing up in a Quaker family didn't save me from a beating if a gang stopped me in a Republican neighbourhood and asked me to identify my religion. I wasn't beaten for being a Protestant – I was beaten for not being a Catholic. And the same treatment was handed out in Loyalist districts, where I was beaten for not being a Protestant. I found myself fervently wishing that our family had been either Protestant or Catholic, at least that might have halved the risk of getting a beating!

For a while I tried just lying. If I was stopped by a gang in a Catholic district I pretended to be a Catholic. If I was stopped by a gang in a Protestant district then I pretended to be a Protestant. Unfortunately this wasn't enough. You had to *prove* you were either a Catholic or a Protestant! You had to say which school you went to, demonstrate you lived in the right street, recite a Hail Mary, sing a Protestant 'party song' (a 'party song' is a political song with sectarian connotations). On one occasion, when challenged to prove that I was a Catholic, I naively answered, "My father's a priest and my mother's a nun!" Needless to say, that earned me yet another beating.

In fact the whole concept of religion left me deeply confused. My parents' liberal Quaker religion was extremely tolerant and nice – but the downside of that was that it seemed to me to be so vague that nothing really mattered one way or another. There was no preaching or teaching of doctrine. People gathered every Sunday for an hour, and they would sit in silence until somebody felt 'moved by the Spirit' at which point they would stand up and speak whatever was on their mind. I remember one Sunday listening to a very nice well-spoken woman holding forth on how Bob Dylan's song 'Blowing in the Wind' should be adopted as the national anthem of Northern Ireland! It seemed to me that a religion that allowed people to stay a part of it and yet believe any old nonsense that they choose is little better than a religion that leads people to beat up all those who don't agree with them. Either your religion was true or it wasn't. If it was true then surely it was important to believe the right things? But if wasn't true, then why bother wasting an hour every Sunday morning pretending that there was a God or that it mattered one way or another whether you loved your neighbour or hated them?

Besides, if there was a God then why did He allow a place like Northern Ireland to exist? Why allow people to blow up pubs, or shoot policemen, or to beat up strangers who strayed into their areas? If there was a God, I thought, then He would owe Sodom and Gomorrah an abject apology for destroying them so readily yet allowing Belfast to continue festering like an embarrassing sore on the face of the earth.

The funny thing is that the part of Belfast in which I grew up, the Newtownards Road in the east of the city, is Northern Ireland's 'Bible Belt.' On every street corner stands some kind of Gospel Hall, Evangelical Church or Pentecostal Mission. On Sunday evenings there was even a traffic jam as people made their way to Church for the second service of the day. But the religion they presented to a young boy like me was unrelentingly grim. I watched them going into their Churches. They looked so miserable, as if they were going to the dentist. And, coming out, they looked even more miserable, as if they had been to the dentist. I don't ever remember any of those Churchgoers demonstrating anything that remotely resembled the joy of the Lord.

On one occasion, after playing football in the street with my brothers one Sunday afternoon, my step-mother scolded us. "Don't you know you're going to upset the neighbours?" I couldn't understand what she was on about. "Why?" I asked, "What business is it of theirs whether we play football or not?" Her reply was so surreal that it convinced me that I was living in a crazy and confused world where I would never belong. "Some

Christians" she said, "would think playing football on Sunday is a really bad sin – as bad as killing somebody."

What? There were really people that crazy? They thought playing football on a Sunday afternoon was as bad as murder? Yet the craziest thing of all was that my step-mother was correct. Some of our neighbours did believe that. In fact the City Council used to employ a man on Saturday evenings who went round all the children's playgrounds and he chained up the swings and the roundabouts with padlocks, so as to prevent children from desecrating the Sabbath by daring to have some fun on a Sunday.

I've sometimes wondered how differently my life might have turned out if I had been exposed to a more genuine vibrant Christianity. What if I had encountered more joyful Christians who had told me that Jesus loved me and had a wonderful exciting plan for my life? Would it have made a difference?

Probably not. I was already so mixed-up and so locked into a loveless selfishness that, as the Bible says, the god of this world had blinded my eyes so that I would not see the light of the Gospel (2 Corinthians 4:4). In fact, I remember picking up a copy of David Wilkerson's book 'The Cross and the Switchblade.' My step-mother had obviously had some experience with Evangelical Christianity in the past, and there were a few Christian books in our house. I read the book, and found the bits exciting where it talked about gangs fighting on the streets. I liked the idea of being part of a gang – of belonging to something and being able to express how much you despised and hated the society in which you lived. But once the gang members got saved then they became boring in my eyes and I stopped reading the book.

One incident from this time really stands out in my mind. We were driving home one Sunday from the Quaker Meeting House and, as we passed a district in East Belfast called Ballyhackamore, I saw two Teddy Boys standing outside a pub. This was in 1970, yet here were these guys dressed like a throwback to the fifties. They wore the brightly coloured drape coats and drainpipe trousers, brothel-creeper shoes, and bootlace ties. Their hair was greased back with a quiff hanging over the forehead. But what impressed me most was their body language – and that of everybody else around them.

These two guys obviously did not belong. Passers-by stared at them with undisguised hostility. Old women crossed to the other side of the street to avoid walking close to them. But they didn't care! They stood outside that pub and smoked their cigarettes as if they owned that street corner. They knew that they didn't fit in. They knew that everyone else hated them. But they weren't intimidated by that. In fact, they positively revelled in it!

At that moment I knew what I wanted out of life. I wanted to be like those two guys. Not that I wanted to be a Teddy Boy. Far from it, I had no interest in 1950's music. But I wanted to be like them, not only in not belonging, but in flaunting their outsider status in everybody else's faces. I wanted to show the world that I didn't care if I didn't fit in. I was sick of pretending to be what everybody else wanted me to be – whether it was a Protestant, a Catholic, a Quaker, or a son who cared about the rest of the family. I wanted to strut up and down the street like those two Teddy Boys and make everybody else hate me. I wanted to shout out from the rooftops that I rejected religion, and Belfast's sectarian tribes, and everything else that society thought was important. If people thought playing football on a Sunday was so terrible, then I wanted to play football every Sunday for the rest of my life just for the fun of watching them get all indignant. I wanted to swagger along the Falls Road and openly let the gangs know I wasn't a Catholic, to stand on the Newtownards Road and shout "I'm not a Protestant" – but instead of me being afraid of them, I wanted them to be afraid of me.

Yet, in the midst of all this anger and rebellion, I still clung to the hope of something better. A relative bought me a stamp album, but I soon tired of the seemingly pointless pastime of sticking stamps into a book. However, there was something about that stamp album that kept drawing me back. On the back cover was a map of the world that fascinated me. I used to trace the outlines of the different countries and breathe the names of the capital cities to myself. Even though my life was already taking a downward trajectory, I found myself touching the countries on the map with my finger and whispering, "One day I'm going to touch the nations!"

2

A SWIFT DESCENT

In Northern Ireland every child faced an examination at the age of eleven, after seven years of primary education. The Eleven-Plus exam, or 'the Qualifying' as we called it, determined what kind of education you received for the rest of your life. It was a one-off paper that took less than a morning to complete. If you passed, then you were considered future university material and studied at a Grammar School for the next seven years. If you failed, then you were deemed more suited for High School with an understanding that you would enter the workforce once you reached sixteen.

Like my elder brothers before me, I duly passed 'the Qualifying' and was accepted into Regent House Grammar School in Newtownards, County Down. It would mean an extra thirty minutes bus ride to school each day. Of approximately one hundred pupils in our year at Primary School, only eleven of us had passed. The pass rate that year was so low that angry parents besieged the school, demanding that teachers be fired. It meant that none of my friends from the last seven years would be in the same school as me anymore.

Before I started the new term at school, my elder brother, John, warned me what to expect. He said, "When you start at Regent House they'll call you a snob because of the way you speak." (all of the Park boys had retained some traces of our parents' English accents rather than the harsher snarl of the

Belfast accent). "Don't be surprised if they drag you into the toilets and flush your head down the bowl – they do that to all the new boys." I digested this information for a while. Then I came to a decision. It seemed like my childhood had always been dictated by the choices and actions of others. Now was my opportunity to remake myself. I was attending a new school where most people hadn't a clue who I was. It was time to start being the person that I wanted to be.

I practiced on my accent. I tried to make it sound rougher, like a real Belfast kid. On my first day at school I let the mask slip for a moment and mispronounced a word. Another boy laughed at me, so I kicked him in the crotch as hard as I could. Nobody laughed at my accent ever again. I remained on my guard against having my head flushed down the toilet, but the word was out – I was not to be messed with. Reinventing myself, I thought, seemed to be working out quite well.

The two big taboos, both at home and at school, were smoking and drinking. I had been smoking since nine years of age, going out of the house to sneak a cigarette and then chewing spearmint gum to hide the odour of smoke. There were no laws against selling tobacco to minors in those days. Shopkeepers used to open packs of cigarettes and sell them singly to schoolchildren. Now, at twelve years of age, some of us would buy six-packs of beer after school, find a deserted spot in a public park, and experiment with how much we could drink yet still pass ourselves off as sober when we reached our homes a few hours later.

Even though I hated school, it wasn't actually that difficult. Blessed with natural intelligence I found that I could learn stuff quickly and complete assignments without much trouble. In fact, my major problem was that I got bored quickly. Sitting for forty minutes in a class to learn something you had grasped after ten minutes was not conducive to good behaviour. Out of sheer boredom I would begin to act up and disrupt the class. Soon I gained a reputation as a trouble maker, yet at the end of each year I would score top marks in examinations.

There were two passions that were struggling for mastery in my heart at this time. One was long distance running, and the other was rock music. I loved running middle distance races during the track season, and cross-country running in the winter. Night after night I would go on training runs of seven miles or more. On one occasion, in physical education class at school, we were all sent on a four mile run. I completed the run so quickly that the teacher refused to believe I had completed the course, believing I must have cheated and taken a short cut. I was made to go out and run the course a second time!

On another occasion I was at the County Cross-Country Championships as part of our school's Minor Team (under fourteen years old). One of the athletes from our Senior Team (under nineteen years old) was taken ill and they needed an extra runner at short notice. So, due to our coach's desperation, I ended up running a five mile course against young adults. I found the whole thing so funny that I couldn't help laughing as I overtook runners who seemed to be twice my height. "What's a kid doing in this race?" they shouted as I left them gasping in my wake. In the end I finished in the top half of the field and won a medal as our team came in second overall. Sometimes I wondered if I could really become a serious athlete. If I could run this fast while regularly smoking and drinking then what could I achieve if I took running seriously?

But running would take second place to rock music. In the mid-1970's a new phenomenon burst onto the music scene – Punk Rock. I was captivated by the raw aggression and rebellion of this youth movement. Punks, with their spiked and dyed hair, ripped jeans and piercings, captured the in-your-face swagger of those Teddy Boys I had seen years earlier. My training runs stopped. I had found a place where I felt I belonged. I even had a new name! I was known as 'Mr Puke' because of my tendency to vomit frequently and in the most inappropriate places once I got too drunk.

As I spent more and more of my time at punk clubs, gigs and parties, my schoolwork and family relationships deteriorated sharply. My parents were trying to raise four other children, but my disruptive behaviour was dominating the family. Something had to change.

In the summer of 1978, when I was fifteen years old, I got a job on a construction site during the school holidays. We were building barns, storage sheds and other farm buildings. Now I had more money, I was spending more on alcohol, and the rows at home intensified. I decided it was time to run away.

One morning, pretending that I was going to work as usual, I pawned my guitar and record collection and used the proceeds to buy an overnight ferry and rail ticket to London. The next morning I arrived in London's Euston Station with thirty pounds in my pocket and a determination never to go home again. I hadn't a clue where to go or what to do. I tried sleeping that night on a park bench, covering myself with newspapers instead of blankets, but even though it was summer the cold chilled me to my bones.

The next evening I ended up in a bar in Canning Town, a tough area in the docklands of East London. A couple of punk bands were playing there that night and I ended up drinking with some of the band members after the gig. They found out that I was homeless and the band's lead singer and guitarist invited me back to the house where they lived. It was to be my introduction to a dysfunctional lifestyle that was as far removed as could be imagined from the middle class suburbs of Belfast that I knew.

As soon as I arrived at that house in Bell Lane, Hendon, I knew that things were going to be crazy. It was divided into bedsits, with a shared kitchen and bathroom. The landlady lived on the ground floor. She used to supplement her income by smuggling cannabis from Morocco. She would swallow numerous condoms stuffed with the drug, and then let them pass through her body, collecting her waste in chamber pots that sat in her living room. This explained the constant odour of human faeces that permeated the house. On the next floor were two rooms – one occupied by the band's lead singer, and the other by the guitarist and his gay lover. They used to fight constantly, beating each other around their room. When they weren't fighting, their favourite pastime seemed to be shooting the mice that infested the house with an air-pistol.

I occupied the tiny box room on the top floor. The rent was low, but on my second night there I fell foul of the previous tenant, who had been evicted for non-payment of rent. He was outside the front door, mercifully (for me) locked out, screaming that I had stolen his home and swinging a samurai sword around. For several nights in a row he reappeared, drawing pentagrams on the doorstep and calling various curses down on me, until the police came one night and took him away. He needn't have bothered cursing me – I was doing a very effective job of doing that to myself.

At every opportunity I had been drinking heavily. The escape and oblivion that came from alcohol was something that I increasingly craved. The time when I was sober was spent looking forward to my next drink. The only problem, as I saw it, was that money was short, thus limiting my drinking. So I found a much cheaper way of reaching oblivion. I began sniffing solvents.

Carbon tetrachloride is a common chemical used for stain removal or stripping polish and varnish from surfaces. I discovered that I could buy a bottle for less than a pound (that's less than $2 US dollars), pour a few drops onto a cloth, and then place the cloth over my nose and mouth. One bottle could keep me intoxicated for an entire day. Solvent abuse is incredibly dangerous, each episode causes hallucinations that culminate in a juddering shock to the body that makes you feel as if your heart is bursting out of your chest. Sometimes I could hear my heart stop beating, and in my befuddled state I would wonder whether this was the time I would die or whether I would come back to full consciousness again.

For the next two or three months I spent most of my waking time either high on solvents or drunk. At fifteen years of age I was too young to claim welfare payments legally, so I did so under a false name. This was before the computer age, and I figured that by the time the welfare office could receive all the relevant paperwork from Belfast, I would have moved on to another district of London. So I used the name and date of birth of an older boy at school who had once bullied me. I don't know if the term 'identity theft' had been coined in 1978, but that is what it was. In a grim act of revenge I used his name to collect welfare payments and build up a substantial criminal record of petty theft, public order offences, bad loans and unpaid fines.

Occasionally I would earn a few pounds working as a roadie for bands, carrying their equipment into venues and setting everything up. The band I was living with was never successful enough to pay roadies. Although musically challenged, they tried to gain notoriety by courting controversy. They were called 'The Raped' and released a record called 'Pretty Paedophiles.' Every now and again a letter would appear in the music press expressing disgust at them – but in fact these letters were written by their manager in an attempt to generate publicity. They weren't even significant enough to cause genuine offence to anyone.

Eventually my craving for solvents and alcohol became so all-consuming that I had no money left for food or rent. My weight began to drop alarmingly, and I ended up being evicted from my room in the house at Hendon. I wandered the streets of London for a few days, sleeping at night in shop doorways. When the weather turned wet I would shelter during the daytime in public libraries.

Even though my life was sliding downhill on an ever accelerating track to destruction, there was still a stubborn irrational glimmer of hope within me that things could be better. My fascination with other countries continued to grow. I would read books in the library that introduced me to the great writers of other nations' literature.

One day I felt as if I had touched rock bottom. In fact I still had further to fall, but this day still represented a new low for me. I sat on the pavement of Tottenham Court Road and begged for coins. I wasn't seeking to get food, or even alcohol. I just wanted enough coins to buy a bottle of solvent so I could put a rag over my face and inhale some oblivion. As I sat begging, with a piece of card in front of me bearing some hastily scrawled lie of a sob-story, I was two-thirds of the way through reading a book that I had stolen from a library. A well-dressed man stopped in front of me with a kindly expression on his face. I looked up and tried to appear needy and pathetic.

"What's that book you're reading?" he asked. I showed him the book cover. It was 'The Brothers Karamazov' by Fyodor Dostoyevsky. He shook his head in amazement. "There probably aren't even twenty young men your age in this entire city who have an interest in reading that kind of literature. Yet you're begging on the street. Don't you know that God could do so much more with your life?"

"I'm an atheist." I replied, "There is no God." For a moment I thought I had offended him, stopping him from giving to me. But he still dropped a few coins into the box in front of me. I remained begging on the pavement on Tottenham Court Road until I had finished my book, but I didn't follow through with my plan to straight away buy a bottle of solvent. Instead I retraced my steps to the library from which I had stolen that book, and I put it back on its shelf alongside Dostoyevsky's other novels.

Then I went to another shelf and pulled down a big illustrated atlas. I opened it up at a map of the world, and one-by-one I began to touch the outlines of the different countries. "One day," I whispered to myself, "I'm going to touch the nations!"

3

TOUCHING ROCK BOTTOM

After sleeping on the streets for a few nights, I was en route to a punk gig one evening when I met a group of guys from Belfast. They played for one of the more popular Belfast punk bands, 'Rudi,' and had relocated to London to try to seal the recording contract which would help them break into the big time and make a fortune. When they discovered that I was homeless they invited me to move in with them. So once again I had a home – if you could call it that.

Elmhurst Mansions was a row of derelict apartment buildings in Clapham, South West London. Anything less like a mansion would be hard to imagine! Earmarked for remodelling, they had become a target for squatters. At that time property laws in England still retained some vestiges of English 'common law' that stretched back to medieval times. Possession still constituted nine tenths of the law, and if you could prove you had been dwelling in an empty property for at least forty-eight hours then it was classed as your home and you had squatters' rights. Eviction required a court order, and that could take months. So the apartments of Elmhurst Mansions housed a community of misfits who lived, rent-free, on the very edges of the law.

There were six or seven of us living in indescribable squalor in one apartment, while the neighbouring apartment doubled as storage space for the band's equipment and as a rehearsal studio. Rehearsals were always interesting since the band played at full concert volume, which usually prompted squatters from neighbouring apartments to start hammering on the door to scream abuse and issue death threats.

And so we settled into a routine of sorts that was centred around sex, alcohol and rock and roll. We would wake up each day at three or four in the afternoon, the band would rehearse while the rest of us tried to steal a few items of food from local grocery stores, and as the evening drew on we would pool our resources to purchase enough alcohol and solvents to keep us partying until dawn. Occasionally the band would play a gig, or we would travel to hear another punk band at one of London's myriad of music venues.

One of our favourite haunts was the Music Machine in Camden Town. This was a huge cinema that had been converted into a concert venue. It hosted some of the top punk bands of the time, such as 'The Clash,' but also provided spots for many up-and-coming bands. Its chief attraction was that we had discovered how to gain entrance for free – clambering up drainpipes and across roofs before dropping through a skylight into a labyrinth of disused offices and projection rooms at the top of the building. Looking back, I am amazed that none of us got killed. We would invariably be stoned or drunk as we staggered across roofs and jumped over spaces between buildings as if in some nightmarish parody of a police chase from a Hollywood movie.

Often we would gatecrash the backstage area of the Music Machine, rubbing shoulders with the headline acts until security personnel would ask us for our passes and throw us out into the street. I remember getting into a drunken argument with Joan Jett from 'The Runaways' and receiving a punch to the face that knocked me off my feet – the first and only time I've ever been whipped by a girl! On another occasion I bumped into Sid Vicious, bass guitarist with 'The Sex Pistols.' We were both so stoned that we engaged in a comical conversation where neither of us had any clue what the other was saying. In retrospect I can see that Sid cut a tragic figure as he was descending into a pit of addiction and despair. A few months later he would die pathetically alone of an overdose in a New York hotel room while he awaited trial for stabbing his girlfriend to death in a drug-fuelled frenzy. But at the time he struck me as heroic, swaggering defiance to God and to the world to the very end.

The apartment where we lived lacked some of the most basic amenities. We had managed to rig up the electricity supply, by-passing the meter and only sustaining a few minor shocks in the process. But for some reason we could only get scalding hot water from the taps, no cold water at all. This posed a problem when we wanted to cook some dried powdered soup, as the instructions on the pack specified that we should use cold water. Eventually we solved that particular crisis by scooping a pot of cold water from the toilet bowl. Bathing was also a challenge, since we had to fill the bathtub with scalding hot water and then wait for an hour or so until it cooled down enough to be bearable. By that time somebody else had usually jumped into the bath before you! Thankfully this wasn't a problem we encountered too often as none of us bathed or washed with any frequency.

Many nights our drunken partying would end in some kind of violence, either against others in the street or among ourselves. Often we would throw empty bottles at each other in the apartment, so most days we would wake up to find the floors covered with broken glass.

I celebrated my sixteenth birthday by cashing a stolen welfare cheque and splashing out on a forty ounce bottle of vodka. The idea was to see how quickly I could drink it, and I vaguely remember knocking the vodka back neat from the bottle as the rest of my housemates cheered me on. The next thing I remember is waking the next afternoon with an acute sense of disappointment and anti-climax. Had I fallen asleep and missed all the fun? I stumbled into the bathroom and saw that the mirror above the sink was broken, the shards of glass discarded into a wastepaper basket. Then I noticed dried blood all over the floor of the bathroom. Not only that, my T-shirt was covered with dried blood as well! I put my hand up to my face and could feel stitches stretching from the corner of my left eyeball towards my ear. What on earth had happened while I had been sleeping?

I ran and shook some of my housemates awake to try and discover what had happened. Apparently I had gone to the bathroom after finishing the vodka and had fallen asleep while sitting on the toilet. Somebody else had started banging on the door and wakened me, at which point my cocktail of vodka and stolen prescription drugs had tipped me over into a state of paranoia. Imagining that someone was trying to kill me, I tried to climb out of the bathroom window, breaking the mirror above the sink in the process. By the time someone managed to kick the bathroom door down, I was once again unconscious, lying face down on the bathroom floor with my pants round my ankles. The most sensible course of action, at least in the judgment of my drunken housemates, was to leave me where I was, to put the shards of broken mirror in the wastepaper basket, and to carry on with the party.

A few hours later I woke up and tried to pick myself up from the bathroom floor. However, when I tried to take a step, my pants round my ankles tripped me and I fell to the floor once more with my face crashing down on the spears of broken glass in the wastepaper basket. By some miracle the glass missed my eyeball by a fraction of an inch and simply cut the skin between my eye and my ear. Today I look back and shudder to think of how close I came to being blinded or killed, but at the time we all found the whole episode vastly amusing.

On another occasion we were all sniffing solvents together, passing round a bottle of stain remover as our bodies jerked spasmodically in time with whatever hallucinations were tormenting our poisoned brains. I got confused as to whether I was drinking or sniffing and ended up drinking the bottle of carbon tetrachloride! Mercifully someone was still conscious enough to phone for an ambulance so I could be rushed to hospital and have my stomach pumped. It was becoming apparent to all that I was spiralling downwards to a grubby and pathetic end. At this point my 'friends' were taking bets on how long I would live. Nobody gave me more than six months.

Then our hellish and destructive routine was broken up. The slow processes of the courts finally caught up with us and we were evicted from Elmhurst Mansions. A couple of the guys from the band were arrested for various offences and remanded in custody, so the other band members decided to return to Belfast. I found myself back on the streets of London again. I slept in doorways and derelict buildings. Winter was drawing near, and the nights were so cold that I was sure I was going to die. Hunger gnawed at my stomach like a trapped animal. Until that time I never truly understood what real hunger feels like.

In absolute desperation I sank lower than I had ever dreamed possible. I sold my body on the streets for sex as a rent boy. There were plenty of men in London's gay scene at that time happy to pay for 'fresh young meat' in the form of a sixteen year old boy. I hated and despised them, but not as much as I hated and despised myself. I wished I had the courage to die of cold and hunger rather than debasing myself in that way.

Was this where all my rebellion, selfishness and rage had brought me? I had wanted to snarl defiance at the world, but the world had chewed me up and spat me out. I knew I had to get out of London and back to Belfast, but how? I certainly wasn't going to admit defeat and ask my parents for help. I needed to go back on my own terms, with at least an outward veneer of toughness and self-respect. I would rather kill myself than sell my body on the streets again, so where could I find the money to travel home?

The answer came that night as I slept in a derelict house. In one of the deserted rooms I found a wig – a big black curly afro wig. Slowly a plan formed in my mind. I visited a toy store and stole a toy gun. It had a picture of Roy Rodgers on the handle, so I tore a hole in the lining of my jacket so that only the barrel of the gun would protrude. In dim lighting it looked pretty realistic.

That evening I marched into an off-licence in the East End of London (that's a liquor store for those unfamiliar with the British terminology) and, absolutely terrified, stammered out, "This is real! Now give me everything you have in the till!" The guy behind the counter was twice my age, twice my size, and looked tough enough to eat me for breakfast. He coolly stared down the barrel of my toy gun and said, "I have two German Shepherd dogs in the back of the store. All I have to do is whistle and they'll run in here and rip you to shreds."

"Go ahead and try it!" I stammered, "I'll shoot you before they come through the door." At that moment I was so caught up in my role as a tough armed robber that I genuinely forgot that my gun was a child's toy. I gripped the Roy Rodgers grip of the pistol harder, and if he had whistled for the dogs I probably would have pulled the trigger to hear a pathetic 'click!' come from my pocket.

"Bah, it's not worth it!" exclaimed the shop-keeper. He reached into the till and placed a bundle of banknotes on the counter. I stuffed them into my pocket, backed out of the door, and then ran across the street towards a housing estate. Half way across the street something thumped my shoulder and I heard a sound like an explosion beside me. I looked down to see broken glass and liquid on the surface of the road. The shop-keeper had followed me outside and thrown a bottle of whiskey at me. It had missed my head by a fraction. If his aim had been slightly better he would have been a hero!

I was so angry that for a moment I started to return across the road to shoot him. Then I remembered that my 'weapon' was really a child's toy with a picture of Roy Rodgers on the grip. I disappeared into the housing estate opposite and quickly dumped the wig and the toy gun into a decorative flowerpot. Trying to appear calm and unconcerned I strolled towards the nearest London Underground Tube Station, as two police cars raced past me in the opposite direction with sirens wailing.

That night I booked a room in a cheap and dingy bed and breakfast near Euston Train Station. I didn't sleep at all. My heart kept racing in my chest, and every moment I expected the police to break down the door and arrest me. I quickly realised that I wasn't cut out to be a master criminal. But my one and only escapade as an armed robber had served its purpose. I caught the train to Scotland the next day, and then took the Ferry across the Irish Sea.

I arrived back in Belfast feeling irreparably damaged. I carried a secret shame inside me that I thought must seem obvious to anyone who looked closely enough. On the outside I still talked and acted like someone who didn't care what the world thought. But inside I felt like a wounded animal. I wanted to find somewhere quiet to curl up and die. All childish notions about touching the nations had been crushed. I knew I had touched rock bottom and that people don't return from that kind of place. The future offered nothing but darkness and death, and my best hope was that the end would prove to be as quick and painless as possible.

4

RUNNING THROUGH TREACLE

A recurring dream has followed me for thirty years. I find myself back on an athletics track, running a middle distance race. I reach down into my reserves of strength and expect to accelerate away as I did in the past. Instead, it's as if I'm running in slow motion. My legs are heavy, and every step feels like I'm running through treacle. Invariably I awaken bathed in sweat, the bedclothes twisted around my legs.

The two years of my life that followed my return to Belfast were like running through treacle. It was an ordeal simply to wake up each day. Every morning felt like a hangover, irrespective of whether I had been drinking the night before or not. Looking back, I understand that I was suffering from profound depression. At every opportunity I turned to alcohol or solvent abuse to try to lose myself in oblivion, but that just kept making everything worse.

I tried returning home, but that was a disaster. I had done too much, seen too much, to fit into a family environment. I ended up sleeping in the back of Rudi's Ford Transit van parked in a suburb of East Belfast.

One night, at the Harp Bar in Belfast, I met a young girl called Valerie. She was fifteen and I was sixteen, and we shared a mutual physical attraction and a disdain for family and society. We talked about marriage and called ourselves 'engaged.' I managed to find a job as an apprentice electrician and, surprisingly, avoided getting fired for nearly a year. A friend of Valerie tipped me off about an empty apartment on a Loyalist housing estate in Greenisland, on the northern edge of Belfast. So I became a squatter once more, staking my claim to the apartment.

However, Belfast was not like London. It might be part of the United Kingdom, but the dictates of paramilitary private armies were more pointed and swift than the archaic English laws of tenancy and possession. I soon received a visit from a representative of the Ulster Defence Association (UDA), a terrorist organisation responsible for some of the most brutal sectarian killings of the Northern Irish Troubles. He informed me, in no uncertain terms, that if I remained in that apartment for any length of time then I would be 'knee-capped.'

Knee-capping was the paramilitaries' favourite way of enforcing discipline. Its mildest form was known as a 'friendly knee-capping' (now *there's* an oxymoron), which consisted of a bullet in the fleshy part of the calf – painful, but not crippling. But ignoring that warning resulted in a full knee-capping, where the victim was shot straight through the knee joint, shattering bones, muscles and tendons. In some variations a power drill was used instead of a gun. Knee-cappings were usually accompanied by a statement from the paramilitaries to the effect that the victim had been punished for 'anti-social behaviour.' Personally I think it's pretty anti-social to go about shooting people through the knee-caps, but obviously the terrorist godfathers saw things differently from me.

Today you can still see men of my generation in Belfast who walk with a peculiar gait caused by the spring-loaded action of their artificial knee joints. On the positive side, however, surgeons in Belfast came to be acknowledged around the globe as the world-leaders in the field of reconstructive knee surgery!

One of the ironic parts of this episode was that the man who delivered this threat to me was not some stereotypical thug. He was a respectable figure in the community, a town Councillor and an elder in the Presbyterian Church. Needless to say, this only served to increase my contempt for Christianity.

Obviously such a threat, coming as it did from an organisation with so much blood on its hands, needed to be taken seriously. But I had no where else to go. Each night I would lie awake wondering when the gunmen would arrive. One night, after cooking myself a make-shift meal of spaghetti covered in thickly-mixed powdered tomato soup, I was in bed when I heard noises coming from the kitchen of my apartment. It sounded as if broken glass was being removed from a window. I grabbed a steak knife that I kept beside my bed for protection and steeled myself for what was coming. "Come on!" I screamed, "I'll gut the first one of you that comes through the door!" All I could hear was silence. For fifteen minutes or more I waited, clutching the knife, straining every nerve as I listened for the sound of rushing feet. Eventually I summoned the courage to enter the kitchen. I had left the packet of spaghetti leaned against the wall on a work surface, and it had gradually slipped down, allowing strands of dried pasta to cascade onto the bare kitchen floor. I had been in fear of my life and screaming at a pack of spaghetti!

Obviously it was impossible to continue living there for long. Valerie had now turned sixteen and, not surprisingly, her parents were opposed to our relationship. We decided to pool our meagre resources and moved into a dismal rented apartment together in a Republican area of Belfast. The apartment was so infested with cockroaches that the peeling damp wallpaper writhed at night as if it were alive. Neither of us were capable of looking after ourselves, let alone sharing life with another person.

I had thought that holding down a job would add stability to our relationship, but the added income just meant more money to spend on drink. My cravings became so bad that I could no longer function without alcohol or some other toxic substance in my system. I vividly remember going out to a bar one night, leaving Valerie weeping on her own in the apartment. It would have taken me ten minutes to walk to the bar where I'd planned to drink, but I couldn't wait that long. I had to call in at another bar en route and gulp down a drink or two to keep me going until I reached my destination.

On another occasion I was drinking in the Pound Bar in Belfast city centre and, as was far from unusual, drank so much that I lapsed into unconsciousness, slipping off my chair and ending up lying on the floor under the table. A few hours later I awoke to find myself in total darkness and wondered where I was. I had been locked inside a bar for the night! Obviously nobody had noticed me under the table, and the staff had locked up and gone home.

At first I was like a kid in a candy store. I walked behind the counter and began to mix drinks for myself, every imaginable concoction of alcoholic beverage disappeared down my throat. Then a horrible thought occurred to me. What would happen when the staff opened up the bar the next day? Most city centre businesses paid protection money to one paramilitary organisation or another. If I couldn't work out an escape then my knee-caps were history! By this time my unhealthy lifestyle had reduced my body to skin and bones, weighing less than seven stone (that's one hundred pounds). This enabled me to wriggle out through a toilet window into a yard outside. Then I had to scale a wall topped with broken glass and a fence topped with barbed wire. I arrived back at the apartment at six in the morning, and Valerie opened the door to find me covered with blood from cuts to my hands, but mightily relieved to have made my escape. To this day I've wondered if any other alcoholic has actually broken *out of* a bar!

Eventually, to nobody's surprise and least of all my own, Valerie found the courage to walk away from our humiliating lifestyle and returned to her parents. We continued to see each other for a few more months, like addicts that can't let go of their addiction, but there was no more talk of engagement or marriage. Any semblance of stability had long gone from my life, and it seemed pointless to pretend that the future could hold anything worthwhile. To this day it is one of my lasting regrets that I was selfish enough to drag another human being down the path of destruction and degradation that was consuming me. I have no idea what became of Valerie, but it is my fervent prayer that she found some kind of peace, and someone who would treat her with love and dignity instead of using and mistreating her.

I was beginning to suffer from alarming blackouts where whole days disappeared from my consciousness as if they'd never existed. It was like waking up in a strange place with no idea how I'd got there. Once I came out of a blackout to find myself sitting on a bus deep in conversation with a total stranger, yet I hadn't a clue what I'd just said or where I was. Another time I returned to consciousness in a bar just as a fellow-drinker was drawing back his fist to punch me in the face. I had no idea what I had done to provoke him, but I figured I must have deserved it so I just let him hit me anyway. On one particularly frustrating occasion I 'woke up' to find I was standing in a doorway locked in a passionate embrace with an absolutely gorgeous girl. I had no idea who she was, nor what pick-up line I had used to land a girl who was so obviously way out of my league!

For the next few months I alternated between brief tenancies in grubby bedsits and periods of homelessness. I remember one apartment that was so cold in the winter that I ended up prising up all the floorboards and burning them in the fireplace to try to keep warm. Obviously I had to move on from there once the landlord wanted to carry out an inspection of the property!

Another time I lived in a house with a bunch of hippies. They kept a pot of stew permanently on the stove, and everyone was expected to buy some meat or vegetables from time to time and throw it into the pot. I think it was something to do with increasing global harmony through communal living. The only problem was that no-one ever got to the bottom of the pot. It even had cigarette butts in it, and pieces of plaster that had fallen from the crumbling ceiling.

Not only was my life characterised by homelessness and drunkenness, but it seemed to be getting increasingly violent. I had not been known as the kind of drunk that becomes aggressive, but rather as the kind that cries into his beer. Unlike many of my contemporaries in Northern Ireland I didn't enjoy violence. When I was sober I would do anything I could to talk my way out of a fight. This led some of the other guys on the streets to taunt me that I was afraid of a fight. Maybe they were right. Unfortunately this led me, when I was drunk, to compensate by trying to pick a fight with the biggest and baddest person I could find. The end result was that I kept picking fights that I couldn't win, becoming a regular late-night visitor to hospital to have various cuts stitched up.

One morning I woke up in a shelter for the homeless to find the back of my head was stuck to my pillow with dried blood. I had absolutely no memory of what had happened the night before. After I'd managed to detach the pillow from the back of my head, re-opening the wound in the process, I picked up my jacket from the floor beside the bed. But when I tried to put on my jacket, it seemed as if I had shrunk during the night! The jacket sleeves extended six inches past the tips of my fingers and the body of the jacket reached down to my knees. Gradually my befuddled brain comprehended that I must have someone else's jacket. But this jacket must have belonged to a giant! I stand five feet eleven inches tall, but this jacket dwarfed me.

Later that day I caught up with a drinking buddy who told me what had happened. Apparently, after leaving a bar, I had picked a fight with a guy on the street. In time honoured fashion we had removed our jackets to fight, throwing them down on the pavement. He threw the first punch, lifting me right off my feet so I landed on the back of my head – which explained all the blood. Then the police had showed up, so we had grabbed our jackets and run for it. In all the confusion we had each picked up the wrong jacket. What really concerned me was the size of this jacket! I must have picked a fight with one of the biggest men in Ireland. If I felt myself to be so invulnerable as to do that, then my drinking was definitely out of control. However, I did have the last laugh, as I found a ten pound note and a full pack of cigarettes in one of the jacket pockets, whereas I knew without a shadow of a doubt that my own jacket pockets had been empty of anything of value.

On other occasions the violence had no humour to redeem it. One night a group of us were staggering home after a hard night's drinking when we were attacked by a rival gang of skinheads. Thankfully the streets were deserted of innocent passers-by, it being the early hours of the morning. A full pitch battle ensued. Eventually the skinheads retreated, but left one of their number lying injured on the ground. I watched as two of my friends jumped repeatedly on his head, until he was unrecognisable as a human being. The next day I was sitting in a café when I heard on the radio that he had died from his injuries.

I was never actively involved in killing another human being, but that owed more to the grace of God than to any self-restraint on my part. There was a punk known as 'Big Tommy' who was fond of throwing his weight around. One of my drinking buddies, Ben, had a run in with Big Tommy and was determined to get revenge. He took a couple of carving knives from his parents' kitchen, and we waited, crouching behind a wall beside Big Tommy's apartment. We were both stoned at the time and I have no doubt we would have committed murder that night. To this day I thank God that Big Tommy hooked up with a girl that evening and went to her place instead.

Finally everything seemed to fall apart all at once. I had been evicted from my latest apartment in spectacular fashion, when a fight in a bar had escalated into a full scale riot with hundreds of angry youths surrounding my apartment building at midnight and throwing stones through the windows. Valerie had finally had the good sense to sever our relationship for good.

Also I had finally managed to get fired from my job, although it was a miracle I had lasted that long. I had already survived the fall out from an incident where a classic building we were renovating burned down, according to the newspapers due to an 'electrical fault,' causing five million pounds worth of damage. But my next mistake would prove impossible to gloss over. Our company won the contract to rewire recording studios at a television station. As the youngest apprentice on the site it was my job to lock up the tool sheds at the end of the day. But I took the keys home with me by mistake, then went off on an epic alcohol bender that kept me off work for the next four days. None of the electricians could access their tools or equipment, and our work schedule was tightly coordinated with the station's recording schedule. As a result filming had to be cancelled with actors and musicians having to be sent home. This was a public relations disaster for our company and marked the end of my short career as an electrician. I had only myself to blame.

Now I was homeless, jobless, and without any meaningful relationships in my life. I sat on a street corner and assessed my life so far. I was seventeen and a half years old, and I had achieved nothing of worth in my life. Anyone else that had come into contact with me had been debased, degraded and impoverished by the experience. There was no prospect that anything would change in the future. I decided, with a minimum of fuss or drama, that the best course of action would be to cut my losses and end my life as quickly and as painlessly as possible.

But how to go about it? I had an aversion to physical pain. On one previous occasion I had tried to cut my wrists, but stopped after one wrist because it hurt too much! I decided that jumping off a high building would be the best mode of suicide. It wouldn't hurt. Also there was less chance of changing your mind half way – once you jumped you would be past the point of no return.

One of the landmark buildings in Belfast city centre, the ABC Cinema, was undergoing renovations. It was cloaked with scaffolding, and in 1980 there were few safety fences or any security measures such as you might find on construction sites today. I had worked in construction, so it was no difficulty for me to steadily climb the scaffolding until I reached the rooftop. Within a few minutes I was standing overlooking Belfast, that stinking sore of a city that I had detested for so long.

I leaned over the edge and I could see people moving like ants on the street below. There was no fear of death, just a sad resignation over unfulfilled hopes and dreams. I never had touched any nations after all.

As I braced myself to jump something happened. There was no flash of lightning, no choir of angels, but a deep and settled conviction overwhelmed my heart. I knew without a shadow of a doubt that if I jumped off that rooftop then I would go straight to hell.

Where did that conviction come from? I was an atheist, for God's sake! I had convinced myself that heaven and hell were just stories invented by powerful churchmen to keep the masses under their control. I despised Christians as weak-minded cowards who lacked the courage to face up to the ultimate meaninglessness of the universe. Yet here I was, a man whom a few minutes ago had been ready to die, yet now overcome and humbled by the fear of hell. I have no doubt today that what I experienced on the rooftop of the ABC cinema in Belfast that February night in 1980 was the ministry of the Holy Spirit who was sent by God the Father to "convict the world of guilt in regard to sin and righteousness and judgment." (John 16:8)

5

THE HOUND OF HEAVEN

I fled Him, down the nights and down the days;
I fled Him, down the arches of the years;
I fled Him, down the labyrinthine ways
Of my own mind; and in the mist of tears
I hid from Him, and under running laughter.
Up vistaed hopes I sped;
And shot, precipitated,
Adown Titanic glooms of chasmed fears,
From those strong Feet that followed, followed after.
But with unhurrying chase,
And unperturbed pace,
Deliberate speed, majestic instancy,
They beat—and a Voice beat
More instant than the Feet—
'All things betray thee, who betrayest Me.'
(Francis Thompson – 'The Hound of Heaven')

As I stood on the rooftop of the ABC Cinema, the scaffolding around me suddenly seemed much less secure. I had climbed up without any fear of heights whatsoever, but the realisation that hell was real had shattered my bravado. As an atheist I had seen death as the ultimate oblivion, simply a more permanent version of the oblivion and escape that I had been seeking in alcohol and solvent abuse. But now I saw death as an enemy to be feared.

I no longer had the courage to climb down from that rooftop. I was terrified that I might slip, fall and be dashed to pieces on the street below. I grasped the most secure piece of scaffolding that I could find and cried out, "No! I don't want to die! I don't want to go to hell!" Eventually someone on the street below heard my cries and phoned the emergency services. Within the next thirty minutes the street filled with police cars, ambulances, a fire truck and an excited crowd of onlookers.

A huge extendable ladder reached up from the fire truck, and soon a fire officer appeared beside me. He reached out his hand and tried to get me to join him on the ladder. Meanwhile the crowd below were shouting at me to jump!

"No!" I cried, "I don't want to fall! I don't want to go to hell!" The fire officer lost patience and, grabbing me, threw me over his shoulder. Since I weighed less than a hundred pounds, it must have been little different from carrying a large child. The crowd below mocked and jeered me as the ladder descended. I was bundled into an ambulance and taken to hospital.

At hospital the examining doctor began by asking my name. Then he asked me for my parents' names. When I mentioned my father he put down his clipboard and stared at me in astonishment. "You're Dr Park's son?" As a student he had attended my father's microbiology classes, and now his impersonal manner disappeared. "I'm sure we can sort all this out." he said, "Just wait here for a while."

When he returned it was once more as the impersonal disinterested doctor whose duties involved having to deal with lowlifes like me. "I phoned your father," he informed me, "He said he doesn't want anything to do with you." It turned out that none of the alcoholic treatment centres would admit me because, at seventeen years old, I was still legally a child. None of the childcare homes would admit me because I was considered more unruly and violent than most adults. "There's only one place we can put you." I was informed, so I was signed into a psychiatric facility.

I don't blame my father for not wanting to get involved. I had brought so much trouble and strife into our home in the past, and he had a responsibility to try to preserve some sense of order for his other children. My current situation was in no way attributable to any failing on his part. I, and I alone, was responsible for where I was now.

Thankfully I only stayed in psychiatric care for a few days, because everybody else in that place seemed to be nuts and it was driving me crazy! I left carrying a letter stating that I had been discharged and was of sound mind. I've often joked that such a letter is useful to a preacher of the Gospel. There are times that I've shared about Jesus with unbelievers and they've responded by saying, "You're crazy!" I can answer, "No, I'm not crazy. And I've got a letter from the hospital to prove it!"

Just as an aside, one Sunday I shared this story at the North Cleveland Church of God, pastored by Mitch Maloney. After the service one of the congregation came to me and said, "I've got one of those letters too!" He pulled out his Bible and proceeded to turn to the text that says, "For God did not give us a spirit of fear, but of boldness, of love and a sound mind." (2 Timothy 1:7) He was quite correct – every Christian has a letter that certifies they aren't crazy!

As I try to share my story with others, one of the most inexplicable things is why that incident on the rooftop of the ABC Cinema was not immediately followed by a surrender of my life to Jesus Christ. Now I knew that God was real. Now I knew that heaven and hell were to be taken seriously. What possible reason was there to stop me from seeking salvation and forgiveness? In fact it would take another year, almost exactly to the day, until I finally received Christ as my Saviour.

The original sin of Satan was one of pride – not being content with an already exalted position but rather wanting to usurp God. Similarly, Satan tempted our first parents with the enticing prospect that they could 'be like God' (Genesis 3:5). Pride is so bound up with human sinfulness that we are even capable of feeling proud about the things that are most shameful. I had reached a point where I had no home, no job, no relationships of any worth, and no possessions other than the clothes I wore. I had done things that I couldn't bear to think about myself, let alone allow them to be known to others. Surely, of all the human beings that ever walked this earth, I had no reason to be proud about anything.

But, through some perverse trick of the Evil One, even a man who has touched rock bottom is capable of pride. I still despised Christians. I still hated their Gospel. Even though I had demonstrated my utter inability to run my own life, I still baulked at handing the reins of that life over to Jesus Christ. For a full year I fought the claims of the Gospel on my life. Night after night I would argue with myself and others. I would bore strangers in bars by telling them how I wasn't really such a bad person after all. And all the time the hound of heaven pursued me. The Holy Spirit kept prodding my conscience.

One night I was desperate to find a warm bed to sleep in. I figured the best way to achieve this would be to get myself arrested. Getting arrested wasn't too bad at all, providing it was for something minor. You got to sleep in a warm cell for the night, and even received a breakfast. Then, in the morning, you were driven to the courthouse and ordered to pay a fine. You were released again with a promise to pay the fine within twenty-eight days, and then you kept moving to avoid the warrants for unpaid fines. All in all it was much preferable to sleeping on the street.

A light snow was beginning to fall, and Belfast city centre seemed even more grim and inhospitable than usual. I made my way to Musgrave Street Police Barracks. In 1980 Northern Irish police stations resembled fortresses. Many police stations had been attacked by terrorist rockets and mortar rounds. They were surrounded by high fences and barbed wire. At Musgrave Street a sentry box and vehicle checkpoint separated the police station from the rest of the street.

I gathered a few empty beer bottles and began lobbing them at the sentry box. At the first shattering of glass, a machine gun barrel appeared. Encouraged by this sign of life I kept throwing more bottles, but nothing happened. Evidently the cops inside knew exactly what I was trying to achieve, and they had decided to ignore me. I felt overwhelmed by rage and impotence. I couldn't even manage to get myself arrested properly!

So I staggered into the street and lay down in the middle of the road, arms and legs stretched wide. The snow continued to fall. Traffic was sparse as it was now the early hours of the morning, but an occasional car still had to swerve to avoid running me over. "Surely," I thought, "Surely they will have to arrest me now." But nothing happened. I realised that I was so insignificant that the police in the sentry box genuinely didn't care whether I lived or died. I slunk off into the cold darkness of the night, weeping hot tears of rage and shame.

Although Northern Ireland's violent Troubles formed a constant backdrop to my life on the streets, their direct impact on me was somewhat limited. Other young men of my generation ended up committing acts of murder, and many of them lost their lives or wasted away for years in prison. There was never any danger that I would be recruited by the paramilitaries – my loose tongue when drunk would have been a liability to any criminal organisation! But my continuing involvement in petty crime was finally coming to the attention of the paramilitary godfathers. I began to receive warnings, concerning both Republican and Loyalist groups, that I could expect to be knee-capped at any time.

A knee-capping, if the victim received prompt medical attention, was still a crippling and life-changing event. But it was not unknown for victims to bleed to death from the wounds inflicted in this savage method of punishment. I would frequently end up sleeping wherever I happened to fall over in a drunken stupor. I had become used to waking in Republican or Loyalist areas of the city, soaked in my own urine and vomit with no idea how I'd got there. I realised that if the paramilitaries caught up with me at such a time, then there was a real possibility that I would bleed to death before anybody would bother to call an ambulance.

Death had previously held no fear for me, but since my epiphany on the rooftop of the ABC Cinema things had changed. Now I knew that death was not the end. I knew that something lay beyond death that was truly worthy of fear. For the first time in years I began to take steps to ensure my own safety and preservation. I had to get off the streets. Unfortunately my antics over the years had resulted in me being barred from most of the hostels or homeless shelters in Belfast. There was only one place left for me to go – the Salvation Army.

In all my hatred of Christianity, I reserved my fiercest criticism for the Salvation Army. Their uniforms and brass bands reminded me of the motherless Christmases of my childhood. Although they were respected by Protestants and Catholics alike in Northern Ireland, I viewed them as hypocrites. Their public image of compassion and integrity, so different from my sordid selfishness, was too great a contrast for me to bear. The only way I could console myself was by cherishing the notion that they were really no better than me.

Yet, in order to get off the streets and survive, it was to the Salvation Army I had to turn. I accepted their charity with gritted teeth. I determined to be as unpleasant and as uncooperative as possible. It would give me the greatest pleasure to provoke them to anger – to demonstrate that they could be as mean and vindictive as me. The problem was that they kept on loving me. No matter how unpleasantly I behaved, they responded with gentleness and compassion.

To make matters worse, these Salvation Army people had something I had never encountered before. They had the joy of the Lord. I was used to Christians being dour and miserable. It was easy to hate Christians when they locked up children's playgrounds to try and make everyone as miserable as themselves, but these Salvation Army people were a different kind of Christian. I had devoted my life to doing whatever made me feel good. If something promised a buzz then I would take it. Yet these Salvation Army folks did none of the things that I thought constituted a good time. They didn't drink, they didn't take drugs, they didn't fight, and they didn't sleep around. Yet they were obviously much happier than I was! I found myself becoming increasingly jealous of their joy. Perhaps I should check out their Sunday worship service? Who knows? Perhaps I could get some of their joy without having to get Jesus?

The Dee Street Salvation Army hall stood in a solidly Loyalist working class district of Belfast. Dee Street leads from the Newtownards Road to the Harland and Wolff shipyard (where the Titanic was built). The kerb stones were painted red, white and blue, and murals on the gable ends of houses portrayed sinister gunmen from the Ulster Volunteer Force with black balaclavas and Kalashnikovs.

The Sunday I first walked into Dee Street Salvation Army was almost exactly a year to the day from when I had climbed to the roof of the ABC Cinema. It was a cold February night, but inside the hall was warm and inviting and bustling with people. But as I looked around, I felt as if I didn't belong. Everybody seemed happy and nicely dressed. I, on the other hand, was dirty and unwashed. My clothes were ripped and torn. My hair was cut into a Mohican, or Mohawk, shaven on either side with a spiked green stripe down the middle. I could see one or two middle-aged women giving me curious sidelong glances.

Suddenly I began to feel afraid that I was going to mess up these good folks' Sunday worship service. As long as I could remember I had been spoiling things for other people. I had turned our family into a place of chaos. I had destroyed Valerie's life. It seemed like everywhere I went, I left a trail of tears and destruction behind me. I was getting ready to stand up and leave when a grey-haired guy in Salvation Army uniform came over and said, "It's great to see you! I'm so glad you decided to come tonight." He had the broadest smile I had ever seen, and he grasped my hand in a firm handshake.

I sat back in my seat again. Who was this guy? Why was he so pleased to see me? He obviously knew me from somewhere – but where? Was he a friend of my father? I put aside all thought of running out the door. If this guy was so glad to see me then I'd better not upset him by leaving before the service even started.

Later I would discover that Jackie Boyd greeted every visitor to the Salvation Army in that same way. Never underestimate the importance of having Church greeters to welcome visitors. If Jackie had not given me his usual welcome then I would never have stayed for the start of the service – and who can say whether I would ever have had another opportunity to hear the Gospel?

Jackie handed me a hymn book and a Bible. I looked at the Bible with interest. I had a Bible that sat beside my bed in the hostel, but I used to use the pages to make cigarettes. I would pick discarded cigarette butts off the street and open them to salvage the few flakes of tobacco still inside. Once I had collected enough tobacco then I could roll my own cigarette. The pages from a Bible, being extremely thin, worked better for this than those of ordinary books. In the words of Packie Hamilton, another former alcoholic from Belfast, "I had smoked my way through Matthew, Mark, Luke and John."

The Salvation Army Captain that preached that evening was Reg Scott. He made no pretence at being a fancy speaker. In blunt language that I could understand he talked about sin, the cross, and salvation. He made the Bible sound like so much more than a book of cigarette papers. He made me forget my plan about finding joy without finding Jesus. I knew that I needed Jesus, and I had to get things settled that very night.

The tradition in the Salvation Army is to invite unbelievers to walk to the front of the hall at the close of the sermon and to kneel at a wooden bench, known as 'the mercy seat.' I really wanted to respond to this invitation, but something was stopping me. I was embarrassed by my appearance. I didn't want to step out in front of all these respectable people. All their eyes would be fixed on my torn clothing, on my Mohawk haircut, they would see the holes in the soles of my shoes when I knelt down. So I prayed my first ever prayer. I said, "God, I'll make a deal with You. If You're everything that preacher says You are, then this shouldn't be too hard for You. I'll stand to my feet – but You get me to the front of the Church."

I stood up, and the next thing I knew I was standing at the front of the Church in front of that wooden bench. Now, I know that I must have walked. As with any Church, the same with the Salvation Army, people still look at what's happening even when the preacher asks everybody to close their eyes in prayer. If I had floated through the air then someone would have seen it and started shouting, so I know that I must have walked up that aisle. Nevertheless, to this day I don't remember taking a single step. I had prayed my first prayer, and God had answered it!

As I knelt in prayer, a man came and knelt beside me to pray for me. I knew his face. His name was Matt McCullough and he was a policeman! I had spent the last few years running from people like him. But this night he grabbed me by the arm and said, "If you pray this prayer with me, then we will become brothers, joined by the Blood of Jesus!" Matt led me in a prayer of repentance and faith. I felt a release and a joy. I knew that something indescribable was taking place in my heart. I also knew that if this was real then I would spend the rest of my life sharing it with others.

People have sometimes asked me when I first received the call to ministry. My answer is always the same: I was called to ministry the same night that Jesus saved me. As I knelt there in my ragged clothes, worn-out shoes, and my Mohawk haircut, I must have looked the most unlikely candidate ever for Christian ministry. But something miraculous was taking place that Sunday night. God was taking a man who had touched rock bottom, and calling him to touch the nations.

Nick Park

6

THE ROAD TO RECOVERY

It is always easier to tear something down than it is to build something up. Any idiot can smash a window in seconds, but it takes patient skilled work by a glazier to replace the same window. The same is true of human lives. Salvation, of course, is an instant work of grace through faith, and the moment we truly repent and turn to Christ we are saved and assured of eternal life. But learning to live as a Christian, and leaving the past behind, isn't always instantaneous. We've all heard dramatic testimonies of how Jesus touched someone's life and they were never the same again, but sometimes those testimonies fail to recognise the struggle and the process involved in being a new creation.

Even as I left the Dee Street Salvation Army hall that evening, I was wondering if I would mess things up again. Failure and defeat had become so integral to my thought patterns that it was hard to imagine a life of victory or achievement. I knew something had happened as I knelt at the mercy seat, but I was still painfully aware of all of my guilt and shame. While we had been in the service, a shower of snow had fallen. I returned to the hostel and looked out of the window.

Normally the view from that window was of urban decay and squalor. The docks of Belfast no longer bustled with the prosperity of bygone years. Derelict warehouses were surrounded by patches of waste ground. Brick walls topped with broken glass guarded yards filled with bags of rubbish and the occasional dead cat. But this night everything was covered with a new crisp layer of snow. Everything looked different, new and clean. As I gazed over this transformed landscape, I felt like shouting, "That's me!" I realised that all of my moral filth was forgiven. All things had become new!

I've heard converted alcoholics testify how Jesus instantly took the desire for drink from them, but that isn't how it happened for me. I had a long struggle ahead of me. This drug, this poison, was so deeply engrained in my soul that I craved it constantly. I would manage to stay sober for a few days, but then the cravings would become too strong and I would go out and get drunk again. I am so grateful to those Christians around me who kept encouraging me each time I slipped and fell. It would have been easy for them to have abandoned me, concluding that I was not serious about following Christ, but they didn't give up on me. George Hardy, the Captain in charge of the Salvation Army hostel, kept saying to me, "Nick, you might be in the gutter, but you don't belong there anymore."

Eight weeks after my initial salvation experience, things came to a head. I had managed to remain sober for an entire week – something I had not experienced in three years. One of the guys living in the hostel was celebrating his birthday, and several of his friends planned to mark the occasion by going on a 'pub crawl' (drinking in as many different bars as possible in one night). I kept refusing their invitations, but my resolve was weakening. Finally I said, "Alright, but I'll just join you for a drink or two in the first bar. After that I'm going home." I wasn't fooling them and I wasn't even fooling myself. We all knew that an alcoholic can't stop after one or two drinks.

I lost count of how many bars we visited that night. I do remember getting into a fight at one point, but nothing too serious. Finally we had all run out of money, and the bars were all closing anyway. It was a couple of miles walk back to the hostel, and there were eight of us. We were all pretty drunk so we made plenty of noise as we staggered through the streets. We were a mixture of Protestants and Catholics, because when you're a drunk you'll happily go along with any other drunk who might buy you a drink. The craving for alcohol is more powerful than racism or sectarianism.

Somebody had the bright idea of teaching one another 'party songs' from our various backgrounds and traditions. We began by singing songs that celebrated the exploits of the gunmen of the Irish Republican Army (IRA). Then some of the Protestant guys had us singing songs that celebrated past victories of King William of Orange over the Catholic King James in the late Seventeenth Century. Unfortunately we were singing these Protestant songs while we were walking through a hardline Republican enclave known as the Short Strand.

All of this was taking place to a background of some of the greatest political tensions that Northern Ireland had ever faced. The Provisional IRA had long been campaigning for their prisoners in British jails to be afforded 'political status' rather than being treated as common criminals. The British Prime Minister, Margaret Thatcher, was famously intransigent. Her catchphrase was, "This lady's not for turning." It was a classic case of the irresistible force hitting the immovable object.

At first the Republican prisoners refused to wear standard issue prison clothing. Instead they remained naked in their cells and wrapped blankets around their bodies. This was known as 'going on the blanket.' The next stage was the 'dirty protest,' where prisoners smeared their own excrement over the walls of their cells. Still the British government refused to budge. The prisoners began a series of hunger strikes designed to continue to the death. To maximise public sympathy, most of the hunger strikers were in prison for lesser charges than murder.

The first prisoner to go on this death fast was Bobby Sands, imprisoned for illegal possession of a handgun. His case became a cause celebre. He was even elected in absentia, while starving to death, as a Member of Parliament for the staunchly Catholic constituency of Fermanagh and South Tyrone. As Bobby Sands grew steadily weaker it became apparent that neither he nor Mrs Thatcher were going to give way. He was the first of ten prisoners who starved themselves to death. Over one hundred thousand mourners attended his funeral, and his hunger strike is considered by most historians to have turned Sinn Fein, the IRA's political wing, into the political force it has become today.

As Bobby Sands' death approached, in those final hours, a palpable tension settled over Northern Ireland. There would be violent protests, that much was certain. Nobody knew how wild things would get. Some newspapers were predicting that the Province would tip over into full scale civil war. Republican areas, such as the Short Strand, were combat ready. Everybody was on edge, armed and ready for trouble – everybody, that is, except for eight idiotic alcoholics who were staggering through the Short Strand and singing antagonistic Protestant songs.

What happened next was like a scene from a movie. The residents of the Short Strand thought they were under attack from a Protestant mob, and they were ready to defend their community. Young men came charging out of houses armed with clubs, chains, and hurley sticks. I found myself in the midst of the most frightening and sickening outbreak of violence that I had ever experienced. A guy called Eddie, who was standing beside me, was struck across the face with a club. I heard the crack of his jaw shattering, and he collapsed on the street with his head twisted at an impossible angle. I tried to run across a patch of waste ground that was littered with debris and pieces of concrete. I never even saw the blow coming, but someone punched me on the side of the head and I fell headlong onto the ground. I looked up and tried to focus. A young man was standing over me. His hands were raised above his head and I saw that he was holding a concrete block. Then everything went black.

I could feel something sticky on my face. My eyes felt as if they were glued shut. There was a lot of noise around me, but it was muffled and dulled. I could hear screaming and shouting, and the wailing of sirens. Most of all I remembered that awful feeling I would get as a child when I knew I had done something very wrong and I was going to be in a heap of trouble. I knew that this time I had really done it. I was in more trouble than I had ever been in my life, and I really didn't know if I was going to come out the other side of it. I wanted to cry out to God for help, but I knew that I had no right to expect any help from Him. I was reaping the consequences of my own choices and my own actions.

I must have lapsed into unconsciousness again, because the next thing I knew I was still lying on the ground in darkness. All the screaming, shouting and sirens were gone. The darkness felt good, like it was hiding me from those who wanted to hurt me.

The armoured police Land Rovers and ambulances had long gone when a man out walking his dog found me on the piece of waste ground and dragged me into his house. He washed the blood from my face. I could hear a woman screeching about blood on her furniture, and she said she was going to fetch someone. I kept lapsing in and out of consciousness, so it seemed like a badly edited film where you jump from one scene into another without knowing what's happened in the interim. The next thing I knew two men were standing over me. "Who are ye?" they kept asking, "Where are ye from?"

In Belfast it is a loaded question to ask where someone is from. Where you are from tells your questioner what religion you are. It tells them whether you are friend or foe. I couldn't believe this was happening to me again. Only this time the penalty for giving the wrong answer could be a lot worse than taking a beating. Knowing I was in the Short Strand, especially after the riot that had just occurred, I had to pretend I was a Catholic. "I'm from Andersonstown," I croaked. Andersonstown is a large Republican district in West Belfast.

"Where abouts in Andytown?" demanded one of the men, "What street do ye live in? What school did ye go to? Who are your friends?" This was like my childhood all over again. I was out of my depth and I had run out of lies. There was only one course of action to take – I pretended to faint again. But this time I was fully conscious. I was more awake than I'd ever been in my life.

The two men proceeded to argue over me. The guy who had found me wanted to call an ambulance for me, but the other man, obviously connected with the paramilitaries, insisted I was a Loyalist who had come looking for trouble and that I deserved a bullet in my head. As I listened to their argument, I silently prayed. "Lord, if I live through this, I promise You that I will never ever get myself into a situation like this."

The scariest thing about staring death in the face that night was that I had no idea where I would go if I died. My atheist notions about death being oblivion had been blown away over a year previously on the rooftop of the ABC Cinema. But I no longer had the assurance of forgiveness that I had felt eight weeks ago when I had gazed across that snow-covered landscape. I really had meant that prayer from my heart the night I had knelt at the mercy seat in the Salvation Army at Dee Street. But I had a good idea that such a prayer didn't cover me for a situation like this, where I was suffering the consequences of sinful and rebellious flaunting of God's will and commands. I was too new as a Christian to have a clue what an Arminian or a Calvinist was, and I hadn't the faintest idea what Eternal Security was. But I sensed that all bets were off if I died in those circumstances that night!

Thankfully, as you've probably guessed by the fact I lived to write this book, the guy who wanted to call the ambulance won the argument. I still pretended to be unconscious in case I said something to make matters worse. When the medics were lifting me onto the stretcher, he said to them, "For God's sake, get him out of here quickly. I can't guarantee his safety."

When I arrived at hospital I was in a bad way. My head injuries were not life-threatening, but I was in shock at my brush with death. I had never suffered from the shakes in all my drinking escapades, but now I was trembling so badly that I couldn't even hold a glass of water to my lips. A young nurse tried to calm me down. She began by asking me my name. Then she asked me where I lived. This was a problem. The nurse was attractive, and I didn't want to admit to her that I lived in the Salvation Army hostel for the homeless. So I gave the hostel's address. "I live at Two Victoria Street!"

"Isn't that where the Salvation Army hostel is?" she replied. So, yes, I had to admit that I lived in the hostel. Her next question was, "Do they hold Christian services in that hostel?" I replied that not only did we have Christian services, but I had given my life to Christ. "That's wonderful," said the nurse, "I'm a Christian too!" Then she asked the question I was dreading. "So how did you end up here in hospital tonight?"

"I was out drinking and we sang the wrong songs in the Short Strand, so someone dropped a concrete block on my head, and then this guy wanted to shoot me, so I pretended to be unconscious!"

That young nurse didn't get annoyed or argue with me. She just looked back at me, hurt and puzzled that anyone who claimed to be a Christian could behave in such a way. And I really don't know how else I can put this – but at that moment it was as if I saw Jesus looking at me through that young nurse's eyes. I saw the pain that my actions were causing my Saviour.

That was the moment when God set me free from my addiction to alcohol. I realised that it was pointless giving God only part of my life. If I tried to give Jesus fifty percent, or even ninety-nine percent of my life, then I was doomed to fail. It had to be all or nothing. So there in a Belfast hospital, with my head still bleeding and an uncomprehending nurse staring at me, I determined that God would have all there was of Nick Park.

7

BECOMING A MAN OF THE WORD

As a new Christian, I desperately wanted to get to know God better. It quickly became apparent to me that the most effective way to do this would be through the Bible. It seemed pointless to expect God to speak to me if I wasn't prepared to pay close attention to the things He had already revealed to others. So I started to read the Bible, a book of which I was almost totally ignorant. I had no idea about Bible reading plans. Nobody told me that I should start by reading Mark's Gospel, then the rest of the New Testament, and then the Old Testament. I figured that the only place to start reading a book was at the beginning, so I turned to Genesis 1:1 and began to work my way through the Bible.

At this time I was offered a job. It wasn't a difficult job – all I had to do was guard a building at night. The people who offered me that job must have had rocks for brains, given my past of petty crime. In fact, I had once broken into the very building that I would now be guarding! But for a new Christian it was a perfect job. Each night I had to sit in an office for ten hours doing nothing, waiting to see if someone would break in.

I took my Bible into work with me and started reading from the beginning of Genesis, so in effect I was getting paid for reading my Bible each night! I would read the Scriptures for ten hours solid. When I got to a bit I didn't understand, then I would kneel down beside my chair and pray until God gave me an insight and understanding into what I was reading. At first everything went great. Genesis was full of exciting stories, and I was reading them for the first time. I was fascinated by people like Abraham and Joseph. Exodus was pretty fast moving too. But when I got into Leviticus I hardly understood anything. I think I spent much more time on my knees praying for understanding than I did reading the text. There were whole chapters in there about what to do if you have mould growing on your wall! But gradually I began to see the benefit of Leviticus. It gave me a deep appreciation for God's holiness, and how we can't mingle truth with error.

I've always been a fast reader, and so it only took a few weeks, reading and praying ten hours each night, that I reached the end of Revelation. Now what was I to do? After all, I had done the Bible. I didn't understand that you could read the Bible more than once! As far as I was concerned, you read a book once and then that's it. What's the point in reading the same book twice? It's not going to say anything different from the first time you read it.

But I really missed the fellowship with God that I had enjoyed when I was reading the Bible through. So I decided to do something I'd never done before, and try reading a book twice. I went back to Genesis 1:1 and started again. I was amazed. Each time I picked up this book I was still seeing something new within its pages. At first I was worried. Was this some kind of memory problem connected with my past substance abuse? Were the blackouts I had experienced for the last two years merely a symptom of some deeper brain damage? But then I began to understand that the Bible is no ordinary book. It is God's Word! Since God's mercies are new every morning, so is His Word. And I can testify, thirty years later, that I still find something new every time I pick up the Bible.

As I read the Bible I began to long for the opportunity to share with others the things that God was showing me. Even as a child I had always been a loner, and my subsequent lifestyle had effectively torpedoed every relationship that I had ever known. Often I would grasp an insight into God's Word and wished that there was someone I could run to and share it with. As I prayed, I realised that this was actually a call to teach God's word to others. But I had left school with no qualifications at fifteen years of age. How could an uneducated man ever be a teacher? And what Bible College would ever accept a student who hadn't even finished his basic schooling? I hadn't the resources to pay for Night School or anything like that, but I discovered I had the legal right to enter privately for the 'O' level examinations that every pupil in school sat when they were sixteen years old.

So I visited a second-hand bookshop, and bought copies of all the textbooks I could remember from my last year in school. Over the next few months I read each one of those textbooks from cover to cover. Now my Bible reading each night was interspersed with English, History and Mathematics. I sat my 'O' level examinations and at last received the qualifications I should have gained three years earlier if I had continued with my schooling as originally planned. Now I could start thinking about going to Bible College.

Of course study of the Bible is supposed to lead us into an intimate relationship with God, not just to impart academic theological knowledge. It was during this time of intense reading of the Bible that God began to do some amazing things in my life. I realised that reading the Bible produces very practical results.

As I read about Zacchaeus, the tax collector who gave his life to Jesus (Luke 19:1-10), I was forced to consider the issue of making restitution. Zacchaeus didn't just need to be forgiven for his past sins, nor was it enough for him to change his ways. He also had to make restitution to those he had ripped off in the past. I began to pray and ask God to show me how I could make restitution. Immediately the Holy Spirit brought something to my memory.

A couple of years earlier I had rented a television from an electrical store. They had recommended a television that was geared for customers like me who had 'poor financial management skills.' This television had a slot mechanism on the back. The idea was that you had to insert coins in the slot each time you watched television. That way, when the rental was due each month, the company representative simply called round and emptied the cashbox on the back of the television. Unfortunately my problem in those days was not so much poor financial management skills as poor financial integrity. Before the first month was over I had broken open the cashbox to spend the money on drink, had sold the television, and had moved out of that apartment, leaving no forwarding address.

Now the Holy Spirit was prompting me to act upon what I had read in the Bible about Zacchaeus. I realised that I had to go to the electrical store and tell them what I had done. But what if they called the police? With my past record, if I appeared in court again, there was every possibility that I would receive a custodial sentence. It was only after a long inner struggle that I walked through the door of the electrical store and began explaining to the clerk that I wanted to pay them back for a television I had stolen two years earlier.

Thankfully they didn't call the police. Because I was living on a low income, we reached an arrangement by which I would pay them five pounds a week until the total cost of the television had been reimbursed. So, every week when I received my paycheque, I would go straight to the store and pay my five pounds. This was before computers were widespread, so I was given a little payment card on which my five pounds was recorded each week. I could see that it was going to take a long time until the television was paid for, but I had never expected that restitution would be easy. This went on for four weeks. But on the fifth week I was paying my five pounds to the clerk, when a smartly dressed man who was watching us suddenly asked, "What's all this about?" It turned out that he was the area manager for that chain of stores, and he took me upstairs to his office.

"Don't you know we have a company policy to always prosecute thieves?" he barked at me. "What makes you think you can just waltz in here and pay a pittance each week when you've stolen valuable property from us? Anyway, why did you steal a television in the first place?"

So I told him my story. I explained about how I had broken the cashbox because I needed money for drink, and about how I had left that apartment and ended up on the streets. I told him about my experience on the rooftop of the ABC Cinema. I told him about giving my life to Jesus at the Salvation Army hall at Dee Street. I even told him the story of Zacchaeus. It wasn't until I'd finished talking that I realised that I had been talking for hours and the afternoon had turned to early evening. Then that area manager leaned forward and said, "Son, that's the most remarkable story I've ever heard. I'm not a religious man, but I want to do everything I can to help you keep going the way you're going." And at that he took my payment card and stamped it so that it read, 'Paid in Full!'

My Bible reading also helped me address some of the hindrances that stood in the way of becoming a preacher and teacher of God's Word. Thankfully, after I stopped drinking, I no longer suffered the blackouts where I would lose whole days of my life. But I knew that they were symptomatic of some deeper damage to my mind. Solvent abuse is rarely seen as a major drug problem in comparison with high-value drugs such as heroin or crack cocaine, but inhaling those chemicals is still incredibly damaging. Even now, after breaking the habit, I would still find myself stumbling over my words or getting confused at quite simple concepts. This was all the more frustrating since I had once been able to pass examinations and top the class with a minimum of effort. Who would want to listen to a preacher who would lapse into mumbling incoherent nonsense?

Then one day, as I was reading my Bible, I came across the verse that says, "I will restore unto you the years that the locusts have eaten" (Joel 2:25). I felt faith rising up within me as I read that verse, and I determined that it was going to be fulfilled in my mind. God was going to restore the damage that years of sniffing solvents had caused to my brain.

A few weeks later, I had an opportunity to see whether God had responded to that faith or not. I was applying for a new job, and as part of the interview process I was asked to complete an Intelligence Test. As I completed the questions, I silently prayed that I wouldn't make a fool of myself. The tests had to be mailed to England for grading, so I was asked to return for another interview one week later. As soon as I re-entered the office I noticed that my interviewer seemed much less friendly than a week previously. "Do you take us for fools?" he ranted, "What's the point of us paying for these tests to be graded if you're going to pull a stunt like this?"

Uh-oh, it looked like my brain cells hadn't been restored like I had prayed! I was getting ready to defend myself, to insist that I hadn't deliberately scored the test badly, when I suddenly realised that wasn't the problem. The interviewer wasn't angry because I had scored too *low*, he was accusing me of cheating because the score was too *high*. Apparently nobody had ever attained a perfect score in that test, but now I had, so he was concluding that I had cheated. I tried to explain to him about Joel 2:25, but that just made him angrier. Needless to say, I didn't get the job. But I did leave that interview praising God for answered prayer. Not only did He restore the brain cells that had been destroyed by solvent abuse, but He replaced them with better brain cells that left me even smarter than I had been in the first place!

Another hindrance to my goal of becoming a preacher and teacher was a problem that must seem minor and trivial to any reader who has never suffered from this affliction, but will immediately resonate with others. I was prone to bouts of excessive shyness and blushing. It sounds crazy that someone who used to wander the streets in ripped clothes and with green hair should get embarrassed easily, but this was a problem that started after I got saved. As I continued to worship with the Salvation Army at Dee Street, I was painfully aware that everybody else was so much more respectable than me. I tried to learn to fit in. I tried to like the music they liked, and to be interested in the same things, but it just made me even more awkward. I didn't understand it at the time, but I was experiencing that curious interaction of spirituality and culture that comprises Church life. I had crossed the spiritual barriers of sin and unbelief. Theologically I believed the same creed as everybody else in that Church. But culturally I was separated from them by a huge gulf.

If I had only known it at the time, this relationship between spirituality and culture would become one of the defining issues of my future ministry. How can we reduce the cultural barriers that stop people joining our Churches, yet avoid compromising the essential spiritual truths and transformation that are necessary for true discipleship? But in 1981 this all lay far in the future. My very present problem was that I felt like a square peg in a round hole, and as a consequence I was getting absurdly embarrassed.

Every time I attended Church, I would start dwelling on how I didn't fit in. The people around me knew I had been an alcoholic, but there were so many other aspects of my story of which they were ignorant. "If they really knew what I have done," I thought to myself, "They would never sit beside me." I would imagine that everyone was looking at me, and that would cause me to start blushing. The problem with blushing, as anyone who has suffered from this problem knows, is that the more you try to stop yourself, the worse it gets. So I would get progressively redder until my face was nearly purple. By then everybody was looking at me! They were saying, "Look at the guy with the red face."

Even worse, if someone came up to speak to me I would get more embarrassed and tongue-tied. How could I ever become a preacher if I couldn't even *sit* in Church without getting acutely embarrassed? So, once again I turned to the Word of God for answers. There I found my answer in these words, "The righteous are as bold as a lion" (Proverbs 28:1). "That's it!" I said, "I'm having some of that." And God did exactly what His Word said. He took away my embarrassment and shyness, enabling me to speak in front of crowds of thousands with a boldness and a freedom that can only come from God.

It was during this period that I faced a test that opened my eyes to some of the failings that occur among Christians, yet ultimately showed me once more the paramount value of God's Word. To be honest, for a while I walked around with rose-tinted glasses thinking that Christians were just about perfect. I was so busy trying to rebuild my own life, gaining victory over the sins of the past, that I didn't pick up on those aspects of Christian behaviour that were hypocritical. Perhaps it also helped that I was still a bit of an outsider in my new Church fellowship. Nobody considered me to be sufficiently on the inside to share any gossip with me!

I was still living at the Salvation Army hostel, and one night I was hanging around the front lobby and reception. One of the residents returned much the worse for wear through drink, and picked an argument with one of the Captains who ran the hostel. The argument escalated until the Captain, feeling threatened by the drunk's aggressive behaviour, pushed him backwards. The drunk fell straight backwards and his head hit the marble floor with a sickening crack. "Quick!" shouted the Captain, "Call an ambulance."

As we waited for the ambulance to arrive, the Captain said to me, "Now remember, if anybody asks you, you say that he fell by himself." I stared at him, with a hollow feeling in the pit of my stomach. This Captain had personally been very kind to me, giving me great support when I had initially struggled to overcome my addictions. But I had also walked where the drunk had walked. How could I connive in a cover-up by someone in authority against someone who was on the very bottom rung of society? "I'm sorry," I replied, "I'm going to have to tell them the truth."

The next few weeks felt as if everything and everyone was peeling me away from my adherence to Christ. How could I say such terrible things about such a good Christian man? Who did I think should be believed – an ordained minister with a record of serving the needy, or a recently saved alcoholic with a past of petty crime and deception? Why was I trying to destroy this good man's career and reputation? To make matters worse, he and his family attended the Salvation Army hall at Dee Street. They would walk frostily past me without speaking to me.

There was only one thing that kept me going at that time, and that was the Word of God. What was most surprising was that the portion of Scripture that most sustained me was the Book of Leviticus. That's right, the same book that I had struggled to read. The same book that contained whole chapters about mouldy walls. The Book of Leviticus, when taken as a whole, tells us that God is passionate about our holiness. He wants us to be clean, and He doesn't want us to dirty ourselves by compromising with paganism, with the world, or in taking any course of action that is dishonest – no matter how advantageous it might appear to be for us.

The Book of Leviticus taught me that my future had to be reached through telling the truth. Even when it was pointed out to me that, by not backing up this man's story, I would have a black mark against me that could stop me going to Bible College,

I still couldn't tell a lie. As it was, God intervened and vindicated my stance. At a crucial point of the investigation, the Captain broke down and admitted that I had been telling the truth. He moved away from Belfast shortly afterwards, but before he went he made a point of talking with me and encouraging me to continue on the path the Lord was taking me.

8

BECOMING A MAN OF INTEGRITY

"Nick, the police are downstairs looking for you. They have a warrant for your arrest!"

Sometimes we do everything we think we have to do to leave the past behind, but it comes back to bite us anyway. I was still living in the Salvation Army hostel, and continuing to grow in my knowledge of the Word of God. I had started the process of applying to study at the William Booth Training College in London, with a view to being ordained as an Officer, or Pastor, in the Salvation Army. Yet now the police were coming to arrest me?

It turned out that I had been arrested shortly before my conversion for being drunk and disorderly in Belfast city centre. I had been released on bail and ordered to return to court at a later date, but I genuinely couldn't remember the incident at all. Not even knowing I had been arrested in the first place, I had obviously missed my date in court. The police refused to believe me, asserting that there was no way I was so drunk as not to be able to remember. I can only conclude that this had all happened during one of my blackouts. To make matters worse, the police had started poking around and discovered my previous history of unpaid fines.

In all the time I was on the streets I was never sent to prison. I was often locked in the police cells overnight to appear in court the next morning, but somehow I had managed to avoid any real

77

jail time. Now I had given my life to Christ, I was free from alcohol and drugs, yet it looked like I might end up going to prison.

I was taken straight to the courthouse and appeared in front of a judge. At the last moment Captain George Hardy, sweating and out of breath, came running into the court. He had heard what was happening and had run all the way from the hostel to the courthouse. He gave testimony as to how my life had turned around, and at the end of the day I was placed on probation. A year later my Probation Officer brought my case back to the court and applied to have the probation order discharged. She argued that my life had been so dramatically transformed that it was a waste of the State's time and resources to keep me on probation. She told me that this was the first case she had ever heard of in Northern Ireland where a probation order had been discharged early in these circumstances.

The next obstacle to my future was of a different nature altogether. At first it appeared to be a physical challenge, which was to teach me one of the greatest spiritual lessons I would ever learn. Then it would become a temptation disguised as a great opportunity.

One of the ministries conducted by the Salvation Army at this time was in connection with the ongoing IRA terrorist campaign. We had a mobile canteen that was equipped to serve hot tea and soup. Every time a major bomb blast occurred we would drive to the scene and provide refreshments to the rescue workers and to shocked by-standers. It was a practical way to demonstrate the love of Jesus to a divided city.

One night we heard a massive explosion, one that shook all the windows in the hostel. Quickly we prepared the mobile canteen and headed towards the site of the bomb blast. I was in the back of the van, sitting beside a huge urn of boiling water. Suddenly the traffic lights in front of us changed, causing the driver to jam on the brakes. The urn of boiling water, however, had not been fastened down correctly and so tipped over. I found myself trapped in the back of a van and standing in six inches of boiling water. I kicked the back doors open and dived out of the van. There were puddles of rainwater on the street, so I began to roll in them, desperately trying to cool my scalded legs. A Police Officer was on hand, so he ran over and tried to help. He pulled off my shoes and socks, but they stripped off my skin, effectively peeling both legs from my calves to my toes like peeling a banana.

So I ended up spending the next few weeks in hospital. The burns on my legs became infected, necessitating a painful course of treatment. Each day huge carbon pads, resembling giant tea bags, were placed over my burns. The carbon in the pads drew the infection out from the wounds. So far, so good. The problem came the next day, when the pads had to be changed. During the night they would stick fast to the burns, so that they had to be peeled off. Have you ever tried to peel a scab off a cut? This was like peeling off six inch square scabs! The pain was so intense that it took several nursing staff to change my dressings, one to peel off the pads and the rest to hold me down.

After a few days of this I was, understandably, getting rather depressed. As I lay in my bed, a doctor was coming through the ward. He stopped at my bed and asked me why I looked so glum. I explained about my treatment, and how I was dreading having my dressings changed the next day. Then he noticed my Bible in the locker beside my bed. "Are you a Christian?" he asked. That made me smile. I remembered the last time someone in a hospital had asked me such a question. At least this time my presence in the hospital was due to good deeds rather than to a drunken escapade. "Yes," I answered, ""I'm a Christian."

What happened next blew me away. The doctor said, "Then, for goodness sake, stop your whining!" I couldn't believe it. Doctors aren't supposed to talk to their patients like that. He continued, "You believe in hell, don't you?" I nodded. "Well, then, what are you going to do about it? Every day people go into a Christless eternity where they suffer in ways that make your experiences seem like nothing. Your pain lasts for ten minutes or so, and once your wounds heal it will all be over. But their sufferings will continue for all eternity. So what are you going to do about it?"

And then he moved on to the next patient, leaving me dumbfounded. That doctor must have broken every code of conduct for the hospital, but I'm glad he did. That was just the revelation that I needed. I needed to remember that God's dealings with me were not just for my benefit, but that there was a dying world out there.

There is a story told about General William Booth, the Founder of the Salvation Army. He was speaking at one of the first student graduations from his Training College. The graduates were basking in their achievements. Their parents and other relatives were there to show support and encouragement. But General Booth began his speech in an unexpected way. "I wish none of you had come to this College!" There was stunned silence. The General continued, "I wish I could have given you a much more effective training for evangelism. I wish I could have taken you to the gates of hell and let you look inside for five minutes. Those five minutes would make you more passionate evangelists than anything we can ever teach you in a College."

My encounter with that doctor was my equivalent of gazing into hell for five minutes. It gave me a burning desire to dedicate my life to winning the lost for Jesus. It put flesh onto my childhood dreams of touching the nations. Many times I have found myself in ministry situations that seemed discouraging, or where I've wished I was back home with my wife and family. But then I remind myself of that day in the hospital ward, and the determination it gave me to cross any sea or continent if by any means God can use me to win a lost soul for Jesus.

However, as my legs began to heal, other people began to encourage me to consult a lawyer. "You could claim compensation," they whispered, "Injuries like yours are worth tens of thousands." Now, it was true that I was saving money to get to Bible College, and the kind of compensation I could claim for my burns would certainly amount to a tidy sum, but I have never felt comfortable with the compensation culture that treats every mishap or accident as an opportunity to win the lotto at someone else's expense.

In Belfast, at that time, there were individuals who carried a little measuring ruler with them at all times. The law stated that if a crack in a pavement was greater than a certain size then the City Council was liable for compensation if anyone tripped over the crack. So these people would measure all the cracks in the pavement, and as soon as they found one big enough, they would proceed to fall over it and then lie writhing on the ground waiting for an ambulance. Back and neck injuries were particularly popular as these were easily feigned. In one court case it was revealed that a woman suing the Council had already made eighteen similar claims. For once the judge acted with common sense and dismissed the case, commenting that after tripping over cracks in the road surface eighteen times, it was reasonable to expect someone to learn to be a little more careful.

In my case there would have been no hint of fraud. My injuries were painful and severe, and they had obviously been caused by someone else's negligence. All I had to do was to retain a lawyer on a no-win-no-fee basis, and bring a case against the Salvation Army. It wouldn't even cost the Salvation Army anything because ultimately the money would be paid by their insurance company. Most cases like this end up being settled out of court anyway.

That all sounds well and good, but remember that I had been spending ten hours each night reading my way through the Word of God. I knew what the Bible had to say on this very subject:

If any of you has a dispute with another, dare he take it before the ungodly for judgment instead of before the saints? Do you not know that the saints will judge the world? And if you are to judge the world, are you not competent to judge trivial cases? Do you not know that we will judge angels? How much more the things of this life? Therefore, if you have disputes about such matters, appoint as judges even men of little account in the church! I say this to shame you. Is it possible that there is nobody among you wise enough to judge a dispute between believers? But instead, one brother goes to law against another - and this in front of unbelievers!

The very fact that you have lawsuits among you means that you have been completely defeated already. Why not rather be wronged? Why not rather be cheated? Instead, you yourselves cheat and do wrong, and you do this to your brothers. Do you not know that the wicked will not inherit the kingdom of God? (1 Corinthians 6:1-9)

I realise that Christians, and even many Pastors, have become adept at ignoring this particular Scripture. When going to court against another believer promises to be advantageous to us, we engage in all kinds of creative exegesis to convince ourselves that the biblical prohibition does not apply to our particular case. But at the time I knew nothing of such sophistry. I only knew that the Bible clearly forbade me from taking legal action against my fellow Christians.

As I inserted the biblical quotation above, I deliberately included the first sentence of verse nine: "Do you not know that the wicked will not inherit the kingdom of God?" We generally prefer to believe that this refers to what comes afterwards – idolaters, adulterers, homosexual offenders, thieves or drunkards. But if you follow the flow of Paul's argument it also logically links to the preceding comments about believers bringing law suits against each other. How could I possibly attend Bible College, knowing all the time that I had paid my way by deliberately flouting such a clear and direct biblical principle? I recognised that to bring a claim of compensation for my injuries was a temptation to be resisted, rather than an opportunity to be seized.

Ironically this same temptation would raise its head again a year later, when my entrance to Bible College was drawing closer. I was riding a motorcycle through the University area of Belfast when a car suddenly turned across my path. The collision sent me somersaulting down the street, causing extensive bruising but, quite amazingly, no broken bones. My motorcycle was a write off, and I had to hobble around on crutches for the next two weeks. It turned out that the driver was a young student up from the country to study. It had been his first time driving in the traffic of the capital city. The student's father offered to write me a cheque for the motorcycle, but said, "I'll fully understand if you want to sue my son for compensation for your injuries."

Was this the breakthrough in my finances I had been praying for? Maybe now I could get the money I needed to go to Bible College? "Tell me one thing," I asked, "Is your son a Christian?" It turned out he was a committed believer. So, once again I had to follow the biblical instruction and refrain from going to court with my brother.

In the end I gained my money for Bible College the old-fashioned way, by working for it. For two years I worked two full-time jobs. At night I worked as a porter in the Europa Hotel (its claim to fame was as the most bombed hotel in Europe), then during the day I painted the exteriors of houses. I would grab a few hours of sleep when I had the opportunity, and then Sunday would be the busiest day of all. Today people complain at the notion of attending Church once or twice, but at Dee Street Salvation Army we had three services each Sunday, plus two open-air evangelistic meetings, and I taught a class in children's Sunday School as well. I was so keen that even that schedule wasn't enough for me, I used to walk two miles to attend another Church's early morning Prayer Meeting before going to my own Church!

Looking back now it sounds like an overwhelmingly busy schedule, but I was young and enjoying every minute of my new life in Christ. Sure, I could have got to Bible College quicker and easier if I had pursued one of those compensation cases, but I had enough things to be ashamed about in my past. I wanted to go to Bible College with the self-respect of knowing that I was doing things God's way.

As the money began to build up for Bible College I knew I needed to be gaining some ministerial experience right away. So I asked the Captain at the Salvation Army if there was a ministry I could be involved in. He said, "Nick, we've got just the ministry for you!" I was delighted. I was going to have my own ministry. I imagined myself as being like Billy Graham with crowds of people responding to my altar calls. "Your new ministry," continued the Captain, "Is to be the Welcome Sergeant." I hadn't a clue what he was talking about. The Salvation Army uses all kinds of military terminology, and unless you understand all the jargon it can be a little bit confusing at times. Still, I was happy that I had a ministry. I was going to be a Welcome Sergeant!

It turned out that a Welcome Sergeant is a greeter. You stand at the door and shake people's hands. Then you hand them a hymn book and say, "Welcome to the Salvation Army." At first I was less than impressed. I didn't see how shaking people's hands and giving them hymn books was going to produce the streams of converts that Billy Graham saw at his Crusades. But the more I thought about it, the more I realised that this truly was a ministry. After all, where would I be now if Jackie Boyd hadn't given me such a warm welcome on the night that I first darkened the doors of a Gospel Meeting? I decided that I would become the best shaker of hands and the best hander out of hymn books that the Salvation Army had ever seen.

I even practiced! I was living in a shared apartment with some other guys, so I would lock myself in the bathroom. I would practice smiling in the mirror, learning which smiles looked welcoming and which were more likely to scare young children. I would practice different voices, saying over and over again, "Welcome to the Salvation Army." Then I would hear the sound of laughter and realise that my housemates were listening at the bathroom door!

Nevertheless I persisted. There's a biblical principle that says, "You have been faithful with a few things; I will put you in charge of many things." (Matthew 25:21) I began to realise that ministry does not consist of jumping into the most prominent role you can find. Instead you show yourself faithful in what God has given you to do, and then He will open the door to greater things. Every Sunday I kept smiling at people, shaking their hands, and handing them hymn books. And gradually I began to get opportunities to share my testimony, or even to preach.

One aspect of integrity that was very important to me was in the area of sexual morality. I was deeply ashamed of my behaviour prior to my salvation, particularly the way in which I had used women as objects of gratification. The Bible declares that the marriage bed should be kept pure (Hebrews 13:4), so I was anxious to make sure that I would not make any mistakes in this area as a Christian. I prayed for God to lead me to the woman that He had in mind for me as a partner for life and for ministry. Finding an attractive woman was not a difficulty, nor was finding an attractive Christian woman. But finding an attractive Christian woman with a calling to ministry and the patience to take on a project like me – now that was much more of a challenge!

I met a young lady called Janice Dodds who was planning to attend the William Booth Bible College, but she was going to study there one year before me. Janice was extremely gifted musically, in fact the first time I saw her was while I was still living in the hostel and she was part of a musical team that came to minister to the homeless. I liked what I saw. She was attractive, had a call on her life to full-time ministry, and I liked her laugh and sense of humour. Her parents had been in pastoral ministry for many years, so she understood the challenges of Christian leadership.

I wanted to ask Janice out on a date, but I was terrified of being rejected. I think, looking back, that I had suffered so many disappointments in my life that I found it hard to believe that the good things that happen to other people could also happen to me. I waited until just a few weeks before she went to Bible College, that way I figured that if she said "No" then I at least I wouldn't keep bumping into her for the next year, and so be reminded of how I'd made a fool of myself.

I spent days working out how I should go about asking her out. This sounds crazy, given my past exploits, but I had no idea how to ask a girl to go on a date. I had only ever hooked up with girls when I was extremely drunk, and I could never remember quite how it happened. So I phoned Janice one night and explained that I had been asked to preach in a little Church on the next Sunday, but they had no musicians. Would she come with me and play the piano? She explained that she was sorry, but that she had already agreed to be at a service elsewhere that Sunday. "OK," I said, "Then to make up for my disappointment, will you come out for dinner with me one night next week?" I couldn't believe it when she said "Yes."

We had dinner together in a restaurant and then went to see the musical 'Godspell.' It was in the same classic theatre which I had worked on and which had been gutted by fire following that 'electrical fault.' It was also right beside the ABC Cinema where I had once climbed to the rooftop with the intention of committing suicide. I decided that neither of those stories would be suitable for sharing on a first date! At the end of the evening I walked Janice to her bus-stop and we gave each other a chaste good-bye kiss. I knew right at that moment that I wanted to marry her, but I thought I'd better not tell her that for a while in case she thought I was crazy.

After she travelled to London to study at Bible College we kept writing to each other. It looked like this relationship was going somewhere, so I travelled across to visit her. I had a little 100cc motorcycle, which I took to Scotland on the Ferry, and then rode five hundred miles in the depths of winter to London. She said she wanted to go somewhere exciting, so I took her to a soccer match to watch Arsenal play Leicester City. There aren't many men who can honestly say that they remember the details of a date twenty-seven years later. But I can still remember that Arsenal came from behind, scoring twice in the last five minutes to win 2-1!

As I walked her back to College, and prepared to embark on another five hundred mile ride to catch the Ferry home, I thought things were going well. But, unbeknown to me, Janice was having doubts. She had met young Christian men in the past who did not share my post-conversion determination to live a pure life. She was used to them making physical advances that she would have to repel. While she was relieved that I hadn't tried to climb all over her on our dates so far, she was also beginning to wonder if I was really attracted to her at all. Maybe, she thought, I was secretly gay! I was blissfully unaware of this as

I rode my little 100cc motorcycle northwards through the driving rain, but I was in danger of losing the woman I loved because I was being so careful to behave like a gentleman.

Thankfully for me, Janice's friends at College soon added a bit of much needed perspective to allay her fears. "Of course he's interested in you," they laughed, "You've found a man who will ride one thousand miles on a motorcycle just to go on a date with you!"

To this day I am so glad that Janice and I were committed to maintaining biblical standards of purity as we developed our relationship together. Before I proposed to her, I had to reveal to her some of my sexual exploits from the past. I didn't want them to be a deal-breaker further down the line. Thankfully she was more interested in our future than in my past. For the next three years we refrained from sexual relations until our wedding day. I have never regretted that, and I believe that has been an important foundation for the mutual love and trust that has kept us married for twenty-five years – and still going strong.

Today it sometimes seems as if young people, even those in Christian homes, view sexual abstinence as hopelessly idealistic or old-fashioned. Sexual experimentation and sex before marriage have become the norm. In many Irish cities the numbers of children born out of wedlock each year exceed those born to married couples. Yet we must understand that integrity cannot be compartmentalised. If we lack integrity in our sexual relationships then it is hopeless to expect that we will demonstrate integrity in finances or in ministry. God is a God of restoration and forgiveness, and more than anyone else I understand that He can take a filthy corrupted heart and make it clean again. But we need to teach our young people that their purity is something precious, worth preserving and valuing.

9

BECOMING A MAN OF THE SPIRIT

For three and a half years, from the day I had yielded my life to Jesus Christ, Bible College had been my goal. Now that I had arrived in London, I had to start thinking differently. Bible College was not meant to be a goal. It was meant to be a preparation for what would come next. Over the next two years I would make some good friends in College, but I think I missed many opportunities to prepare myself adequately for ministry. That was not the fault of the curriculum or the tutors, the problem is that I was not very teachable.

Before I left for College, an old lady in Belfast had said to me, "Don't let them change you, over there in London." I had replied, "Don't worry, I won't let them change me!" And I think my biggest failing over the next two years was that I lived up to that promise. With the arrogance of youth, I thought that I knew it all. I thought that I was going to sail through College and then save the world!

One thing that did have to change was my Belfast accent, the same accent that I had worked so hard to acquire to avoid being bullied at Grammar School. One afternoon the entire body of students were taken to Speakers' Corner, near London's Hyde Park. Speakers' Corner, as the name suggests, is where anyone can stand up on a soapbox and speak about whatever they choose. All kinds of political radicals and spokespersons for different religions give speeches, while a noisy crowd heckles and interrupts them. It is not a place for the faint-hearted. Each of us had to mount the soapbox and share our testimonies. When it got to my turn, I was amazed that no-one was heckling me. People were just staring at me with their mouths open. At first I thought that they were overwhelmed by my power and anointing. Then I realised that they hadn't a clue what I was saying. They couldn't understand my accent! I had to learn to soften the way I pronounced words, and to slow down.

On another occasion, after being in College for about two months, all the students were taken to Soho, in London's West End. We sang some songs of testimony in Leicester Square, and then we were ordered to disperse into the crowds of pleasure-seekers and theatre-goers to witness to unbelievers on a one-on-one basis. I had been looking forward to this. For two months I had been studying theological and philosophical arguments to prove the existence of God. In my arrogance, I believed that I was fully equipped to argue anyone I might meet into an acceptance of the Gospel.

The first person I tried to speak to soon punctured my pomposity. He was a Professor in Theology from a very prestigious German university. He was not born again, in fact his views on the Bible were extremely liberal, but his knowledge of Theology and Philosophy was such that my well-constructed arguments soon dissolved. I quickly had to retreat back to the rest of the students with my tail between my legs!

A few minutes later another student returned to the group. He was my best friend in College, a Scottish guy called Bobby Deans. Bobby had a similar testimony to myself in that he was a converted alcoholic. He knew that God was calling him to witness to others in that lifestyle, and was studying to be ordained as a Salvation Army Officer so he could work as a Captain in hostels for the homeless. Bobby had an extremely strong Glasgow accent, so strong that sometimes you felt you needed subtitles to understand what he was saying. I looked at Bobby. If I had struggled so much with all my well-constructed arguments, then what about Bobby who hadn't appeared to have prepared for this night at all?

"How did you get on, Bobby?" I asked him.

"Och, great!" he replied, "I led two people to the Lord."

I stared at Bobby. How on earth? What evangelistic technique had Bobby studied that I had missed? Had he some wonderful gift in apologetics that I hadn't noticed? "So, Bobby," I asked, "How did you do that?"

"I just told them what Jesus has done for me."

I think Bobby Deans taught me a lesson that day that was more valuable than anything I ever learned in Theology class. It is impossible to argue someone into the Kingdom of God. Whatever great arguments you think you have prepared, you will always encounter someone who knows more about that subject than you. But when you start sharing your testimony with someone, at that moment you become the world's greatest expert on that subject, because nobody knows your testimony better than you do. I'm reminded of the man born blind who was healed by Jesus (John 9:1-34). The Pharisees tried to trip him up by drawing him into a theological discussion about who Jesus was – but he just kept saying, "This one thing I know, once I was blind but now I can see." And because of that they were unable to refute his testimony.

It was while I was at Bible College that I began to sense God drawing me back to Ireland. This was a surprise, since I had been happy to leave Belfast behind, and the Salvation Army system was such that after ordination you would expect to be appointed to pastor Churches in England or Scotland. But now I was feeling this intense burden, not for my home of Northern Ireland, but for the independent Republic of Ireland to the south.

The vast majority of people in the Irish Republic would have been born Catholic, and in 1985 a very large number of these were still practising. Seventy percent of the population still attended mass every Sunday, the highest level of religious observance anywhere in Europe. The Salvation Army, at that time, had virtually no presence in the Republic at all. I had thought of Bible School as something necessary to get ordained, and then I would be sent to pastor an existing Church. But now I found myself thinking seriously about the concept of Church Planting.

Even though I had never studied Church Growth or Church Planting, I understood the powerful role played by culture. I remembered how, when I first got saved, I had struggled to truly become part of the Church. I was so determined to leave my past behind that I had learned to talk like the rest of the people in the Church, to pretend that I was interested in the same things as them. I had taken on board the quasi-military language and structure of the Salvation Army because it was the only expression of Christianity I knew, and it was a lot better than where I had been in the past! But now I found myself facing some disturbing questions. What about people who weren't prepared to learn the language and traditions of an alien culture? How were those people ever going to be assimilated into the Church?

I imagined what it would be like to plant a new Salvation Army Church in a town in Ireland that had never known any religion other than Catholicism. Most of the Salvation Army traditions dated back to Victorian England. How many of those traditions would be useful in such a new location? How many of them would be hindrances, to be better jettisoned than taking the time to explain them? Without knowing what I was doing, I was engaging for the first time in Contextualisation – working out how to present the Gospel in a relevant cultural form. The problem was that I couldn't handle the answers to my questions. If I was to truly present the Gospel in the most effective way in an Irish context, then it would involve dropping virtually every distinctive that makes the Salvation Army what it is. I wasn't prepared to face the implications of this, so I quietly suppressed the call I had felt to the Irish Republic. The Salvation Army was the instrument God had used to save me, and I couldn't conceive of Christian life and ministry in any other context.

At this time Janice had made friends with some Charismatic believers who shared with her about the miraculous gifts of the Holy Spirit. She was excited by the fervency of their faith and experienced the Baptism of the Spirit for herself, but I felt threatened and defensive. Once you think you've got your faith all figured out, it's hard to acknowledge that you might still have something to learn.

In May 1986 I graduated from the William Booth Training College and was ordained as an Officer, or Pastor, in the Salvation Army. Janice had already graduated and been ordained twelve months earlier. Three weeks later Janice and I were married in Belfast and, at the end of our honeymoon, we threw ourselves into our new duties pastoring a small Salvation Army

Church in Leicester, England. Both marriage and pastoring were harder than I had anticipated.

The Church was composed predominantly of retired people, most of them female. We had two Sunday services, a midweek women's service, and an over-sixties club – and it seemed that the congregation in all these services were pretty much the same people. I tried to inspire them with plans to launch a city-wide revival, holding all-night prayer meetings and doing my best Billy Graham impersonations. They looked at me as if I had two heads and reminded me not to forget to draw up next month's rota for who would provide the flower arrangement each Sunday.

Unfortunately, the disconnect between my ideal and reality also extended to our marriage. I had this notion that if two people loved each other enough then they would sail through a life of wedded bliss without having to work at it. I had already failed at every relationship in my young life, and I wanted to make Janice so happy that she would find all her life's yearnings and desires perfectly satisfied in me. She couldn't even complain about bad weather without me saying, "But you should be happy – you're with me!"

It makes me laugh when I hear people use that phrase about a honeymoon period wearing off. We spent most of our honeymoon arguing and making up. In reality we were two young people who loved each other deeply, who both had strong opinions, and were learning how to be married. At first we used to have some fearsome arguments, but we learned to be patient with one another. We have now been married for twenty-five years and I can honestly say that our love and passion for one another has deepened and blossomed over the years. We love each other more today than we did on our honeymoon.

We served that congregation in Leicester for two years, but it was very much a maintenance ministry whereas my heart was to pioneer something new. I would read in my Bible about the vibrancy and power of the Early Church, but nothing I was seeing in my ministry matched up with that. I kept asking myself why the Church that I was seeing every day was so different from the Church that I was reading about in the Bible.

Gradually I realised that ministry, which had been my heart's desire since the day of my salvation, was becoming a chore. I was spending my time on stuff that I didn't enjoy, that brought me no sense of fulfilment, and which didn't appear to be doing much to further the Kingdom of God. Yet I could see no way out. I believed that serving as a Salvation Army Officer was God's will for the rest of my life, and I began to feel trapped. I would see older ministers who were tired and burned out, and I asked myself if that would be me and Janice in thirty years time.

And then God did something wonderful. Out of the blue he baptised me in the Holy Spirit. I wasn't even seeking this experience. I was simply praising God one day, thanking Him for saving me, when I realised that my vocabulary was too limited. I was saying stuff like, "God, You are so good." But God is so much more than good! In frustration I cried out, "Lord, I need to praise you adequately. Please give me the words to praise you!" That was when God filled me with the Spirit, and I began to speak a language I had never spoken before. At first I was horrified. I tried to put my hands over my mouth to stop the words coming out. I didn't believe in this! But I couldn't deny the inner witness of the Holy Spirit.

The charismatic gifts of the Spirit, while not expressly forbidden, were certainly frowned upon in Salvation Army circles.

We had no wish to continue as a disruptive or rebellious influence within that denomination. For Janice and I to exercise charismatic gifts in the Church where we were pastoring, or indeed in any other Church we might be moved to, would only have caused confusion for them and frustration for ourselves. I began to think again of Church Planting, and which of our denominational traditions would prove to be cultural hindrances. With great sadness, and a lot of reluctance, we came to realise that it was time to leave the Salvation Army.

We left without bitterness or rancour. I will always be grateful to the Salvation Army, for without them I doubt if I would even be alive today. When I was on the street and needed someone to show me the love of Jesus, it wasn't the Pentecostals that were there – it was the Salvation Army. To this day we have many friends and family who are still part of that movement, and it is always a pleasure for me to be able to minister in their meetings.

Leaving the Salvation Army was not only saying farewell to a denomination. They were our employers. They owned the house in which we lived, even the pots and pans in our kitchen. Janice was eight months pregnant, and I was jobless, when we went to live in one room of her grandmother's house near Manchester. The first thing we had to do was find a new Church. We read an article in a local newspaper about a little Church in Leigh that had prayed for a dead baby, causing the child to be restored to life again. We visited the Church and loved the fervency and faith of the people. It quickly became our new spiritual home.

I found a job selling life insurance. There was no basic salary, as I just earned commission on the policies I sold. But it turned out to be the ideal job for that point in our lives. With God's help I found I could sell enough policies quickly to make a living, and that left us more time to get involved in the life of the Church. It was an exciting time for me, learning to step out in the gifts of the Holy Spirit. We saw God touching people's lives through prophecies and miraculous healings.

It was there that our first daughter, Kirsty, was born. I will never forget standing in the delivery ward at Bolton General Hospital and holding this new life in my arms. I reflected how the little boy who had promised never to love anyone ever again had now become a man who was feeling more love than anyone could ever imagine for this tiny baby in his arms. Kirsty has grown up to be a beautiful, intelligent and compassionate young woman who brings us great pride and joy. Loving her as a father has helped me understand that love is always a risk, you open yourself up to the possibility of getting hurt, but it is infinitely preferable to not loving and not being loved.

For me, becoming a man of the Spirit was not just about ministry. Nor was it just about spiritual gifts and the miraculous. It was learning that my highest calling was to be a husband and a father. It was about learning to truly live my life for others and to forever break with the egotism of the past.

When I die, the most important thing will not be the number of Churches I've planted, nor will it be how many people remember the sermons I've preached. Nobody will care what councils or committees I have been elected to, nor what academic degrees permitted me to put letters after my name. What will really matter is that my wife knows that I was a good Christian husband to her. The only eulogy I want to be offered is that Kirsty will be able to truthfully say, "My Dad was a good father, and a man of God."

Nick Park

10

THROUGH THE FIRE

Janice and I continued to grow in our walk with God. The little Church we had joined affiliated with the Assemblies of God, and I soon became Assistant Pastor. It was a time of great growth, with new people getting saved every week. The Senior Pastor had a vision for evangelism that motivated and stirred the people. There were trials and setbacks, of course. Vandals broke into our little Church building and burnt it to the ground, but each attack seemed to cause further growth. We pushed ahead with plans for a new building. Then we outgrew the new building and started thinking even bigger.

I continued to sell life insurance, to help pastor the Church part-time, and I also continued my education. I was able to complete both a Bachelor's and a Master's degree in Theology, studying late into the night to complete my courses. My studies focused on Church Growth, Church Planting and World Missions. I began to find answers to the questions that had troubled me about the role of culture, and making Church relevant to unbelievers. I understood the principle of Contextualisation that had shaped my thinking at College when I had wondered what changes would need to be made to plant new Churches in Ireland.

Most of all, my old desire to touch the nations began to burn brightly once more. I realised that this persistent idea, impressing itself on my mind even when I was a confused child and a

101

teenage atheist, was a genuine manifestation of the grace of God. I was enjoying my life and ministry, but I knew that what I was doing in that Church was not God's ultimate plan for my life. He was preparing me for something. I couldn't yet see fully what that something was, but I knew it was connected with Church Growth and Church Planting, and I knew it was going to enable me to touch the nations.

Janice was expecting our second child, and we were full of excitement at the prospect of our growing family. But her ante-natal scans caused some concern to the doctors. They reported that the baby's head seemed too small, and there was insufficient fluid surrounding the child in the womb. In the end Janice was rushed into hospital and our second daughter, Grace, was delivered by emergency section weighing just two pounds and thirteen ounces. She was placed in a special care unit. We couldn't even pick her up and hold her – we could simply press our hands against the glass of the incubator and pray for her.

Over the next few months, doctors carried out a battery of tests to determine what was wrong with Grace. Eventually they diagnosed an incredibly rare condition called Familial Dysautonomia, or Riley's Day Syndrome. Basically Grace's autonomic nervous system didn't work. This regulates so many of the things that our bodies do without us even thinking about it. When Grace cried no tears flowed. She would shiver when she was hot, and sweat when she was cold. Most seriously, her swallowing was uncoordinated, so every time she tried to swallow food, some of it would go into her lungs, potentially causing life-threatening pneumonia. Strangely, this condition usually only occurs where both parents are fully Jewish, yet neither Janice nor I have any Jewish relatives.

Eventually we were allowed to take Grace home, but she required round-the-clock care and attention. Feeding her was an ordeal. We would have to tightly wrap her in a sheet, pinning her arms to her sides. Then we had to insert a tube into her throat and down to her stomach. Obviously this would cause an instinctive reaction to gag and pull the tube out, which was why her arms would be pinned to her sides. Then we had to slowly pour milk down the tube. Often she would be screaming the whole time, and frequently Janice and I would be in tears too. This whole process took about thirty minutes, and it had to be repeated every four hours. We were to continue doing this for the next four and a half years.

Caring for a disabled child is immensely exhausting even under the best of circumstances. It is much harder when you are also trying to care for another young child, help pastor a Church, sell life insurance, and study part-time. Frequently Grace would be hospitalised, meaning everything else had to be planned around feeds and visits. Sometimes the insurance sales were insufficient to pay our bills, and I would take on extra work in warehouses at night, or driving a taxi. Janice and I would pass each other like ships in the night, often too drained even to talk to one another.

One of the hardest things for me to take was the whole issue of divine healing. We would frequently see people healed in our Church services, including some truly astounding miracles, yet our own child remained sick, no matter how often we prayed for her. Evangelists would come to our church, lay hands on our daughter, and loudly prophesy that she was healed. But the next day the evangelist would leave town, while we continued to care for a severely ill child.

I will never forget one incident. Grace was in hospital on Christmas Day, so a male nurse came round the wards in a Santa suit and a white beard, giving presents to all the sick kids. He stood at the bottom of Grace's bed, and she looked at him. She was connected to a ventilator to help her to breathe, so was unable to speak. I cannot describe the impotence we felt as parents, as she desperately tried to say 'Santa,' but couldn't because of the tubes in her throat. I walked out of the ward and punched the hospital corridor wall so hard that I couldn't hold anything in my right hand for several days.

Looking back it is hard to understand how I found the time, but I had the opportunity in 1992 to take a missions trip to Czechoslovakia. After the collapse of the Berlin Wall and the Soviet Union, there was a great need for teaching and pastoral training in the Eastern Bloc countries. I was thirty years old, and I had to apply for my first ever passport. I had been nursing a call to touch the nations, but I had never travelled outside the British Isles. That trip to Czechoslovakia, teaching in a number of different Pentecostal Churches, made me feel like I was right in the centre of the will of God. I began to plan and coordinate other missions projects from our Church.

Personally speaking, my life was in a place of chaos. The demands of caring for Grace meant that Janice and I rarely spent quality time together with each other or with Kirsty. We had recently moved house and financially things were really stretched. Ministry-wise, things were really moving. The Church had grown to a place where we were negotiating to buy a disused high school, and I was really enjoying teaching in the local Church and coordinating missions projects. It looked as if I really was going to have an opportunity to touch the nations.

Then God called me to Ireland. I would find myself continually mulling over what it would take to plant Churches in the Irish Republic. Would people accept the Gospel from a Northerner like me? How could I start a new ministry with a disabled daughter and no financial resources? Would my going to Ireland seem like a betrayal of that Church in Leigh, particularly when they were stepping out in faith to purchase a huge new property? Anyway, where in Ireland could we go?

I was reminded of a quotation from my Salvation Army days. General Booth once said, "Go for souls – and go for the worst!" So where would be the worst place in Ireland? What part of Ireland would seem so inhospitable to evangelism that if we started a Church there, then people would know that it was possible to start a Church anywhere else in the nation?

I thought of the times when we would travel home to Ireland for holidays. We would catch a Ferry from Wales to Dun Laoghaire, just south of Dublin. Then we would drive northwards to visit Janice's parents in Belfast. Each time we made that journey, we passed through the town of Drogheda. It had always seemed to me to be a particularly grey and depressing place. I did some more research, and discovered that Drogheda had a dark and bloody history. After the English Civil War, Oliver Cromwell had invaded Ireland to root out Royalist sympathisers. The siege of Drogheda had culminated in one of the most infamous atrocities in Irish history, with wholesale slaughter of innocent people. One of the major streets in Drogheda is still known as 'Scarlet Street' because of the river of blood that ran through it that day.

Also, just outside the town was the site of the Battle of the Boyne, the slaughter that sealed the victory of King William of

Orange over the Catholic King James, ensuring that England remained a Protestant nation. Today, over three hundred years later, sectarian divisions are still perpetuated in Northern Ireland as Loyalists march to commemorate the Battle of the Boyne. On the very night that I had nearly lost my life in a riot in the Short Strand district of Belfast, the song we had been singing that sparked the riot spoke of 'the green grassy slopes of the Boyne.'

In 1993 Drogheda suffered from high unemployment, high rates of cancer (many suspected this was caused by nuclear waste from an English power station just a short distance across the Irish Sea), and a phenomenally high incidence of teen suicides. Young men regularly became so overwhelmed by the hopelessness of life that they threw themselves into the Boyne River and drowned. To make matters worse, a notorious terrorist from the Irish National Liberation Army, Dominic 'Mad Dog' McGlinchey operated out of Drogheda. He was responsible for supplying the weapons for a particularly barbaric attack where gunmen had travelled several miles to attack a Pentecostal Church during Sunday worship, killing three of the church elders.

So, when it came to finding the worst place in Ireland to start a Church, Drogheda looked to be the winner! Obviously you don't take such a step on a whim or a notion. I had to know for certain that God was calling us back to Ireland, so I prayed and asked Him to speak to us in an unmistakable way.

We were hosting a guest speaker in our Church, an Australian guy named Brian Houston. Today Brian is known throughout the world as the Pastor of the Hillsongs Church in Australia. But in 1993 nobody had ever heard of Hillsongs. 'Shout to the Lord' hadn't even been written yet! We just knew we had some Australian guy coming to preach. I didn't get the chance to speak to Brian before the service, so he didn't know who I was. He certainly didn't know that I was Irish. As he preached that night I would just have looked like any other English person in that congregation.

Imagine my surprise, then, when Brian called me out and began to prophesy over me. To be honest, I was expecting it to be like so many of the generic prophecies you hear in Pentecostal circles, "God loves you. He has a great plan for your life ......" But Brian's first words caught my attention instantly, "God is calling you back to your homeland." Now I was all ears. How did he know that *this* wasn't my homeland?

The prophecy continued, "And God is going to put on you the same spirit that He put on St. Patrick. To plant Churches, and to touch a nation." Incredible! Patrick was the patron saint of Ireland, who first brought Christianity to our land. There was no longer any doubt in my mind – we were going to Drogheda!

At first our Senior Pastor was very supportive of our plans. I had enjoyed working with him, and I was eager to continue our association. But then he began to insist that I should follow a particular methodology in Ireland, one that I knew stood little chance of success. My studies had convinced me that just trying to reduplicate an English or American model of Church in Drogheda was never going to work. I tried to convince him that my determination to do things a different way did not mean I was being critical or disrespectful of him, but our relationship deteriorated. We had several long discussions in which various arguments were presented to dissuade me from going to Ireland. One that I particularly remember was, "If you go to Ireland then what will happen to all your plans to be involved in world missions? You'll be hard pressed just to survive in Ireland, let alone to think about going anywhere else." I remember thinking that this could well be true. It did seem that going to Ireland could be a step backwards from my dream to touch the nations. However, none of that could change my conviction that God was calling us to Drogheda.

Nevertheless our Senior Pastor still very generously allowed me to take a short-term mission team from the church in Leigh to Drogheda for a week's evangelism to help kick start the new Church. We booked a room in the Linen Hall Bar for a week, and preached the Gospel to a noisy crowd of teenagers. Unfortunately one of those teenagers picked my pocket, stealing my wallet, which contained the return tickets for all our team. In order to replace the tickets I had to spend all the money I had raised for the Church start-up costs. So now we were trying to plant a Church with zero financial support.

At the last minute we had decided that Janice and the children would stay in England for a few months longer. Grace was really sick again and needed specialist treatment in hospital. Even so, this was probably one of the stupidest decisions I have ever made as a Christian. The frenetic life we were living, hardly seeing each other and taking turns to sit with our daughter in hospital, had eroded our trust and intimacy. There was little genuine communication taking place between us, so we never talked about how both of us were hurting so badly.

Also, unbeknown to me, leaders in the Church in Leigh had been persuading Janice that I was stepping outside the will of God in going to Ireland. I am grateful for everything I learned as part of that Church, and from that Pastor. He helped me know what it is to walk in the power of the Spirit, and I know I was not always the easiest person to work with. But now things turned sour. They told her that I was an arrogant and headstrong individual who had rejected the authority of the Senior Pastor. They told her that I was too immature to be in charge of a new Church, that I would never be more than 'a good right hand man' to someone more talented and anointed. All of this, combined with existing strains in our marriage, caused her to seriously doubt whether God really had called us back to Ireland.

Today, when interviewing prospective missionaries, I would never allow someone to travel to another country unless their spouse is one hundred percent supportive of their calling. Anything else is just asking for trouble.

In March 1993 I stood on the dock at Dun Laoghaire and waved goodbye to the short term team as they returned to Britain. I had no money, no supportive Church, no Church building, and I wasn't even sure how much of a marriage I had. It had been a long time since I had felt so alone.

11

THE DAY OF SMALL BEGINNINGS

One of the major lessons that I've learned over the years is that God has a whole army of people out there who are just waiting to bless you. I love the Scripture where God says to Abraham, "I will bless those who bless you, and will curse him who curses you, and all nations on earth will be blessed through you." (Genesis 12:3) Have you ever noticed that those who are to bless you are in the plural, but he who is to curse you is in the singular? That means that God has appointed more people to bless us than the Devil has appointed people to curse us!

Of course the key qualification for meeting these people of blessing is that you are in the centre of God's mission and purpose. If God's plan is to bless the nations through you, and you keep that vision before you at all times, then you are in the safest place you can possibly be. I often think of the three young men in Scripture who were thrown into the fiery furnace for refusing to worship the king's idol (Daniel 3:1-30). To everybody else, that furnace looked like the deadliest place in the world, but for them it was the safest place in the world, because the Son of God was waiting for them in the midst of the flames.

Even when I felt all alone in Ireland, God had already appointed people of blessing. Not because I was His favourite, or His pet, but because I was a carrier of His vision and purpose. The flip side of that, of course, is that those who attack the carrier of God's vision and purpose end up cursing themselves.

I have thought long and hard about whether I should put this next paragraph into print, but I think it's important enough to include, even though some may misunderstand it and accuse me of making exaggerated claims as to my own spiritual importance. As I look back on God's dealings with me over the last thirty years, I see a remarkable pattern. Every time somebody has set themselves to attack me, lie about me, or scheme against me, they have not only failed, but they have ended up suffering extreme consequences. I have seen ministries collapse, marriages end in divorce, denominational leaders fall in disgrace, and strong young men contract life-threatening illnesses. At times this has both awed and frightened me.

Am I claiming that Nick Park is somebody special? Absolutely not! I am a very fallible human being and, at every stage of my ministry, I have looked around and seen plenty of people who are better qualified than me to do what I'm doing. But I do believe that the vision I have carried has been something that was birthed in the heart of God, so those who sought to destroy me were, in a very real sense, also attacking the vision of God. This also acts as a warning to me. If I ever become the kind of person, through sin or arrogance, that would besmirch the vision God has entrusted to me, then I should expect my fall to be fast, painful and very public!

Some of the people of blessing that God sends our way are there just for a season, and then they move on. Others become lasting friends and continual sources of life and encouragement. One early person of blessing in Drogheda was Bill Southard. Originally from Wales, Bill had married a local woman and settled down just outside Drogheda. He had a vision to establish a telephone helpline, tackling head-on the problem of teen suicide.

He had gathered some teenagers around him and was touched by our week of outreach in the Linen Hall Bar. He suggested we join forces. Bill rented some store-front premises on the quays beside the River Boyne, purchased some tables and chairs, and installed a pool table. We ran it as a drop-in centre with a weekly worship service. The sign above the door read 'Christian Helpline' but I don't think we ever managed to get a phone line installed.

More teenagers began to attend. Sometimes I would walk the streets at night, stopping to talk with groups of young people drinking on street corners, and sharing my testimony. Some of then gave their lives to Christ and began coming to the centre. One thing that was very obvious was how the Roman Catholic Church still had a great deal of control over people's lives. It seemed as if teenagers could be involved in crime, alcohol, and drugs without anyone seeming worried, but as soon as they started coming to our centre then the priest would warn their parents, and the parents would pressurise the teens to steer clear of 'the Born Again's.' There was even a rumour spreading through the town that we sacrificed goats during our services!

Bill's wife died tragically of cancer, and he took more of a backseat in the running of the drop-in centre and our meetings. Eventually the landlady cancelled our lease and we were left with no meeting place. But Bill generously allowed us to keep the tables and chairs to use once we could find another premises. Bill would remain as a person of blessing, and as a worker in the new church, for a further eight or nine years. Ultimately we disagreed over the direction of the church, and Bill moved on. But I will always be grateful to him, and pray God's blessings upon him, for his kindness and generosity in those early days.

By this time Janice and the children had come over to Ireland to join me, but we were still experiencing huge problems in our marriage. Sometimes I wondered if we were really going to make it. Because of Grace's worsening medical condition, we had to live in Belfast, close to specialist hospital facilities. I hated being back in Belfast again, and having to drive eighty miles to pastor the teenagers in Drogheda. We still had no place to meet, so I was desperately trying to keep our little group of believers together.

This was the point at which God brought another two people of blessing into our lives. Noel and Agnes Joyce lived in Monasterboice, just outside Drogheda. Raised as devout Catholics, they had received the Gospel and were filled with the Holy Spirit. They began to hold Bible Studies in their home. One of the people who came to that Bible Study was a member of the Church of Ireland (Episcopalian). Agnes remembered that Pope John XXIII had said they should concentrate on what united them to other believers, not on what separated them. So what, she wondered, did Catholics and Protestants have in common? The answer, of course, was the Bible! So, because of that one lone Church of Ireland man in their midst, they determined to lay aside both Protestant and Catholic traditions and to go solely by what the Bible said.

The first time that they met, they had no experience in how to conduct a Bible Study. Noel offered everyone a glass of whiskey, and then they began reading the Bible and discussing what it might mean. Soon more people began attending, and the local priest was berating them for being 'black-hearted Protestants.' By the time I arrived in Drogheda, Noel and Agnes had built a prayer-room in their back garden, and every Sunday it was full of people gathering to praise God and to study the Bible.

It would have been easy for Noel and Agnes to have felt threatened when I turned up in Drogheda with a vision to plant a Church. But they were unhesitatingly supportive. They owned a clothes shop in the centre of Drogheda, and offered us the basement of their premises to use as a Church. Later, as our Church would grow and draw worshippers from many of the surrounding villages, Noel and Agnes would stop their services and encourage people to come to us instead. They have never expressed any resentment over this – in fact they have unfailingly exemplified what it means to be people of blessing. I count myself privileged to call them my friends up to the present day.

We painted the basement that Noel and Agnes had provided for us, fitted a carpet, and got ready for our re-launch. Many of the teenagers were still being hassled by their parents for coming to Christian meetings so we decided on a neutral kind of name. They could say to their parents, "I'm going to the Solid Rock Centre," and their families just assumed it was some kind of rock music venue! As we prepared our building, I discovered that part of the concrete floor was uneven. I asked Noel about it, and he told me that there was an ancient bricked-up well on that spot.

That made me think of something. I went out into the alley outside and discovered an old plaque on the wall. It said that at a well near that spot, St Patrick baptised the first Christians in Drogheda in 443 AD. Immediately I was reminded of Brian Houston's prophecy. He had said that God would put on me the same spirit that He put on St. Patrick. Now here we were, over fifteen centuries later, planting a Church on the very spot where Patrick had brought Christianity to Drogheda. I felt as if I was standing on holy ground! We all need those moments when God reminds us and assures us that we really are in the centre of His will.

And how we needed that encouragement! We had opened the Solid Rock Centre in January 1994, but our numbers were few. Janice and I were still struggling in our marriage, and Grace's condition was no better. Sometimes, as I drove from Belfast to Drogheda, I would feel overwhelmed by pressure and a sense of failure. I remember, on more than one occasion, pulling over at the side of the road and breaking down in tears, asking God to give me the strength to continue.

I didn't understand it at the time, but I was learning about one of the most necessary qualities required by a Church planter. It might not sound very spiritual – but sometimes you need to be as stubborn as a mule. Sometimes you just need to keep on going, never knowing when you're beaten.

Finances were continually tight, so I supported our family by working in an onion warehouse. It had to be the worst place imaginable to work. All day long I stood over a huge table of onions, picked up a few at a time, checked they were as close as possible to two pounds in weight, and then dropped them into a bag. To this day I can unerringly tell whether a two pound bag of onions is underweight or not! Every time a forklift truck ran over a loose onion, we would all be crying. My clothes stank of onions, my hair stank of onions, it didn't matter how many times I washed my hands – the smell of onions kept emerging from the pores of my skin.

Sometimes Janice would pick me up from the warehouse and we would drive straight to Drogheda. As we drove I would struggle out of my work clothes and change into a suit. Then I would preach, but even as I reached out my hands to pray for people they would fall to the floor. It wasn't the Holy Spirit – it was the smell of those blasted onions!

Ever since we had left the church in Leigh, I had longed for spiritual oversight and covering. I strongly believe that spiritual authority only operates when you are accountable to someone else. I have never seen the point of people building independent ministries under their own names. God called me to be a blessing and to touch the nations, not to establish Nick Park Ministries Inc!

Jesus once met a Roman centurion who needed a miracle. This military commander said, "I myself am a man under authority, with soldiers under me. I tell this one, 'Go,' and he goes; and that one, 'Come,' and he comes. I say to my servant, 'Do this,' and he does it." (Matthew 8:9)

What is striking is that the centurion did not describe himself as a man *of* authority, but rather as a man *under* authority. He could only exercise authority, and expect obedience, because he was himself accountable to a higher authority. This same principle applies to many areas of life. If I buy a police uniform from a fancy-dress store, then I can try to order people about as much as I wish, but in reality I have no authority. The uniform only confers the power to exercise authority when the person wearing it is duly appointed by the higher authority of the State.

It is striking that some of the ministers who demand the greatest obedience from their Church members are themselves answerable to no-one. I did not want to walk in this kind of hypocrisy, therefore we quickly applied for the new Church in Drogheda to be joined with the Assemblies of God in Great Britain and Ireland. The problem was that the denomination's

Regional leadership in Northern Ireland were wedded to a very traditional model and style of having Church. In the words of Paul Reid, Pastor of the Christian Fellowship Church in Belfast, they were 'like Presbyterians who spoke in tongues.'

We were trying to build a Church in Drogheda that could reach out to unsaved people from a Catholic background. I had figured out long ago that we could not effectively do that by adhering to Salvation Army traditions, but it would be equally impossible to do so by following Northern Irish Protestant traditions. I was looking for spiritual fathers that would understand what we were trying to do and give us the benefit of wisdom and experience. What I found was continual frustration as the Regional Superintendent exhorted me to build a clone of how he thought Church should be.

Sometimes the interference seemed so petty that I felt I was majoring in minors. For example, I realised that celebrating mass was the centre of Roman Catholic worship. Indeed, for a devout Catholic to take communion at another Church is often considered as a statement that they have left Catholicism and converted to that Church. When the President of Ireland, Mary McAleese, visited a Church of Ireland she partook of communion to emphasise that she was the President of all the people of Ireland, not just the Catholics. Because of this she was publicly rebuked by the Catholic Archbishop of Dublin. He accused her of having denied her Catholic faith by taking communion in a Protestant Church.

Most of the people who were coming to our Sunday services were interested in the Gospel, but were still very much checking us out. For us to have celebrated communion in those Sunday services would have prematurely forced them to make an 'us or them' choice. So we decided that we would celebrate communion with our committed members at a midweek service. We wanted this to be more like the fellowship meals that were shared by the Early Church in the First Century. So we gathered on a weeknight, shared some pizza and fellowship together, and at the end of the evening we very reverently brought out the bread and the wine, prayed over them, and celebrated communion together. It was a beautiful and touching moment, and we all went home thanking God for sending the gift of His Son to die on the cross for us.

I had explained to my Assemblies of God Superintendent exactly what we were doing, and he nodded sagely. Imagine my surprise, then, when at our next Regional ministers' gathering, he criticised our Church for 'making a travesty of holy communion.' "These young people," he said, "Use pizza instead of proper communion bread to demonstrate their rejection of everything that we stand for. If this Church is accepted into the Assemblies of God then I will resign as Superintendent. Communion should be celebrated at eleven o'clock on a Sunday morning. Anything else is a denial of our Pentecostal heritage."

In vain did I protest that we used bread for communion just like any other Church. I would be remembered forever as the heretic who used pizza to celebrate communion. It was hard for me to understand whether this opposition stemmed from genuine ignorance of what we were doing, or from a malicious dislike of anyone that did anything innovative.

Our Church in Drogheda continued to grow slowly, but it was hard work. Janice and I were seeing healing in our marriage, but it was hard work. The onion warehouse just about brought in enough money to pay the bills, but it was hard work. Caring for two young children, one of whom was desperately sick, was hard work. Looking for spiritual fathers and instead finding Pharisees was hard work. But we persisted in the calling God had entrusted to us. We even began planting a new Church in Portlaoise, in the midlands of Ireland.

We were just about making it, but sometimes we felt that the slightest wave could rock the boat and send us under. What we didn't know was that we were about to face a virtual tsunami.

12

I'LL PRAISE YOU THROUGH THE STORM

June the 14th 1994 would be our eighth wedding anniversary. I was scheduled to drive to the new Church plant in Portlaoise, and then I had to drive on to Cork to preach there the following day, so we decided to celebrate our anniversary a day early. We were renting a house on the seafront of Bangor, County Down and the sunshine was reflecting prettily off the waves.

That afternoon we took Kirsty and Grace to the beach. Taking Grace anywhere was an ordeal. Her lung capacity had diminished significantly due to repeated bouts of pneumonia, so we had to carry oxygen tanks wherever she went. But she was doing well. It had been eleven months since her last hospitalisation, the longest she had remained out of hospital in her life. As we watched our two daughters paddling in the waves, it was easy to believe that things were going to get better. That night we went to a restaurant and, over a beautiful meal, reviewed some of our shared memories and experiences of the last eight years.

The next day I drove down to Portlaoise. This was before cell phones were in common use, but after the service I was called to a phone. It was Janice, and she sounded worried. "Grace is sick again. My Dad's driving over to take her to hospital. You'd better come home straight away." I wasn't

overly concerned. We had been in this situation dozens of times before, but for Janice's sake I thought I'd better drive home.

It was a four hour drive to the Royal Victoria Hospital in Belfast, even after breaking all the speed limits. There was no need to ask for directions, we'd been here so often that I knew the children's wards like the back of my hand. I looked around, but couldn't see Grace or Janice anywhere. I asked a nurse where they were, and was ushered into a waiting room. A minute or two later Janice came in and knelt beside my chair. "We lost her," she said, "Her little heart just couldn't take the strain anymore."

We'd been warned over four years earlier that this day could come. I'd had four years to prepare for this, but it still blindsided me. I could hear a sound in my ears like a rushing wind, and I felt as if the floor was falling away underneath me. It was like being transported back in time to the day that I heard of my mother's death. But this time, even though the pain still hurt just as bad, I knew that it is better to love someone and lose them than never to have loved at all.

"Would you like to see her?" Janice asked. When I picked up Grace's body her skin was already waxen and cold. She was just two months short of her fifth birthday, but, due to her condition, was as small as a normal two year old. As I held her in my arms, it was as if every voice in Hell was crying out to me, "Where is your God now? You've trusted Him, but now look how He's rewarded you!"

As Janice and I left the hospital, we drove for a little while. Then we pulled over at the side of the road. We both knew of people who had been through such tragedies, and they had consequently become bitter and angry. We didn't want this thing to make us bitter – we wanted it to make us better. So we did the hardest thing we've ever done. We held hands and began to praise God. We didn't feel like praising God. We felt like just curling up and dying. But, with the tears flowing down our cheeks, we thanked God for His goodness, affirmed our trust in Him, and promised Him that we would continue to love and serve Him.

One of the things that carried us through those dark days was the knowledge that Grace was with Jesus Christ. Although Familial Dysautonomia causes many physical disabilities, Grace's mental faculties were unimpaired. Janice had led both her and Kirsty to Christ, encouraging them to ask Jesus into their hearts. Grace was not even five years old yet, but she had made a conscious decision to trust in Christ. She loved to sing worship songs, her favourite being 'The Lord Reigns.'

A few days later came the funeral. I asked the officiating Pastor if I could have a word. I said, "Some people may look at Grace and see a wasted life. But in fact she did the one thing that is needful for a human being to do – she committed her life to Jesus Christ. Some people may not understand what I am about to say, but it needs to be said. As a father, I would rather it happened this way. I would rather she died before her fifth birthday, yet spend eternity with Jesus Christ. This is preferable to her living to be a hundred years old, making a great success of her life and enjoying world-wide fame, meeting Presidents and Queens, yet dying without receiving Jesus and entering a Christless eternity."

It seems ironic that the two most tragic events of my life have occurred on occasions that should be times of great celebration. My mother died on Christmas Day, and our youngest daughter died on our wedding anniversary. As a consequence, these dates are always a time when sadness and joy are strangely mingled.

In the Solid Rock Church, every time we pray for someone who is undergoing turmoil and tragedy, we ask that God will demonstrate that He is everything His Word says that He will be. For Janice and me, He also demonstrated that His Church is what the Word says it will be. We couldn't face removing all Grace's clothes and medical equipment from our home. In fact we couldn't even face walking back into that house ever again. We stayed with Janice's parents while we found a new home. Some Christian friends and family members went into our old house, packed all our possessions, returned all the medical equipment to the hospital, and got rid of all Grace's clothes. That's the kind of Church we read about in the Book of Acts!

So we saw the Church at her best during our time of deepest sorrow. Unfortunately we also got to see the Church at her worst. A few days after Grace's funeral, there was an Assemblies of God Regional ministers' meeting scheduled. Obviously I would not be attending, my place at that time was at home comforting Janice and Kirsty. But all that day I felt a deep uneasiness in my spirit. Something was telling me that I had to be at that ministers' meeting. Finally I left a weeping wife at home, got in my car and, feeling like the worst husband and father in the world, drove to the ministers' meeting.

As I walked through the door, the Superintendent's face dropped. "Oh," he said, "We didn't expect to see you tonight." After expressing suitable condolences, the meeting continued according to the planned agenda. I was only half-listening to what was being said and began to zone out. What on earth was I doing here instead of being with my family? Then I suddenly realised that they were talking about me. There was an item on the agenda that the new Church in Drogheda should be removed from my leadership and placed under the control of the Superintendent! Suddenly I found myself fighting for the future of our Church. I pointed out that everything we had worked to establish would be destroyed if we were to try to structure a Church of new converts in Drogheda according to the traditions of Protestant Churches in Belfast.

Eventually, in the time honoured fashion of Church bureaucracy, the subject was shelved, to be discussed again at a future meeting. I should have felt relieved, but instead I found myself becoming increasingly angry. The Superintendent had known that I was unlikely to be at that meeting – he had said so himself. So why was an item concerning the Church that I was planting still on the agenda if I wasn't expected to be there? Gradually the enormity of what had just happened hit me. He had planned to exploit the death of my daughter, using my absence to play Church politics.

After the meeting, I confronted the Superintendent. "I used to live on the streets." I told him, "I used to hang out with homeless drunks, prostitutes and drug dealers. But in all my experiences, none of them ever sank to the level of using the death of a child to try to push their political agenda." And that, as far as I was concerned, was the end of my association with the Assemblies of God.

I must stress that these problems were pretty much caused by one man in a prominent position. That man has now gone to be with the Lord, and I thought long and hard about whether to include these details in this book. In the end I decided to include them, because they are an important part of my story, but also because they help explain my fervent dislike of Church politics. I believe in denominations, because Churches with similar beliefs and visions can do so much more when they work together than when they are separate or independent. Also, as I've already stated, I believe it is important for Church leaders to be accountable to godly authority. So denominations can be good. Denominations need leadership, and there are always times when leaders need to make difficult or unpopular decisions. I understand all that, and in recent years I have served in denominational leadership, and have had to play my part in making collective decisions where we had to balance hard realities with what other people expected of us.

But even when we disagree with other believers, there is never any excuse for treating them as your enemy. There is never any excuse for bullying people, or for attacking them on unrelated issues in order to get what you want. We might sometimes honestly disagree as to which course of action is the best for a large number of people, but that is a very different thing from simply following the courses of action that you think will be best for your own ambitions and interests. Even when people hold opinions that challenge and threaten our own opinions, we are still obligated to love them, and treat them with dignity and respect. So that is why I have an absolute horror of people playing politics with the Church of Jesus Christ.

This whole episode also impressed upon me the need for young ministers and leaders to find spiritual fathers, who will encourage them to be both innovative and faithful to the Gospel. There is a balance between just letting people do what they feel like, and controlling them to do things exactly the way you would do them. Now that I am grey-haired, I am always drawn to those leaders who think outside the box and use creative methods to share Jesus with others. Sometimes I like to just spend time with them, to affirm them and let them know that I'm a fan of what they're doing.

To this day I have good friends in the Assemblies of God in Britain, and in Northern Ireland, who are fine men and women of God and are reaching their cultures with the Gospel in many creative ways. Also, the Republic of Ireland now has its own arm of the Assemblies of God which, under the skilled and anointed leadership of Gary Davidson, has become one of the leading Church planting agencies in the nation. But, back in 1994, that all lay the future. I had to start looking for a new spiritual home and for new spiritual fathers.

Sometimes men and women react to grief in different ways. Janice had the good sense to grieve deeply and openly. I just worked harder. Maybe it was because I have lived in too many environments where, in order to survive, you have to act tough and to suppress your emotions. The more places that I could find to go and preach, the less I had to think about the yawning emptiness that is left behind by the death of a child.

Maybe if I had worked less and prayed more, I would have avoided making some of the mistakes I fell into. Some believers in Bangor, County Down, most of whom had previously been in the Church pastored by the Assemblies of God Superintendent, invited me to start a Church there. On the face of it, it seemed to make sense. We needed some financial stability, and, in contrast to working with new believers in the Republic who were taking time to grasp the concepts of tithes and offerings, these were more mature Christians who were eager to support our ministry.

If I had been praying more at that time, then I would probably have realised that this 'opportunity' was not in line with where God had been leading me. My calling was to touch the nations and to plant Churches in the Irish Republic. What was I doing trying to start a Church in a Northern Irish town where there were already dozens of Evangelical and Pentecostal Churches? Also, the only thing that had previously stopped Janice and I from moving close to Drogheda was the specialist hospital care provided by the British healthcare system that Grace had required. Now there was no reason to remain living in Northern Ireland, yet here we were settling into a new home two hour's drive from Drogheda. I was about to learn the vast difference that separates a good idea from a God idea.

If I thought the new Church in Bangor could distract me from my grief over Grace's death, then I was in for a rude awakening. In fact the life of that Church was very similar to Grace's life. It started poorly, managed to exist for a short time on life support, and came to a premature end. I tried everything I knew to make it work, everything I had learned from my Church Growth studies, but God's anointing was never on it. I remember feeling such a failure when we finally admitted defeat and closed the Church. There's something about Christians that makes us remember other people's failures much more readily than we remember their successes. Today, if you were to visit Bangor and talk to some people who remember me, the first thing they would remember would be the Church that failed. Yet that experience also taught me one of my greatest lessons.

I was wallowing in my very public failure. Perhaps part of my reasoning in accepting the invitation to start that Church had been an idea that those who disliked my methods of Church planting were watching, and I would show them! Well, I really showed them. I showed them that, without the grace of God, I haven't a clue how to plant a Church! But as I berated myself, I felt the Holy Spirit leading me to turn to a Scripture. I read, "I will build My Church, and the gates of Hell will not overcome it." (Matthew 16:18) At first I didn't see how that helped cope with my failure. The Holy Spirit prompted me to read it once more. Then once more. Finally I began to get what God was saying to me. The Scripture hadn't changed!

I might have failed, but Jesus will still build His Church, and it will still stand victorious. So the key question I had to consider was this: Who was I doing all this for? If I was doing it for me, for my own reputation and glory, then my failure in Bangor was a very bad thing. But if I was doing it for Jesus, then my failure had not affected the final outcome by even one iota. That revelation totally transformed the way I looked at success and failure.

I was painfully aware that we needed to be under some godly spiritual authority. But where could we find people who would love us and support us without playing politics? The answer was about to come from a most unexpected source.

In 1994 many of the Pentecostal denominations in the UK worked together in an evangelistic campaign. I believe it was the late Wynne Lewis, former pastor of Kensington Temple in London, and Superintendent at the time of the Elim Pentecostal Church, who came up with the idea of the JIM Challenge. Jim was an acronym for 'Jesus in Me' and the campaign was supported by billboards and advertisements in newspapers and on radio.

As part of this campaign, a black Gospel band from the New Testament Church of God in England visited Northern Ireland. I got to know John Grey, a Pastor who travelled and sang with the band. He agreed to return later that year with another band and help us evangelise in Drogheda, Portlaoise and Republican West Belfast. There were virtually no black people living in Drogheda at that time, so the visit of John and his team caused a sensation. We tried to go out for a burger, and people were following us down the street and taking photographs!

The events were a great success in terms of people coming to Christ, although they just about cleaned us out financially, and left us totally exhausted. We had a wonderful concert in Belfast on Saturday night in a bar in Andersonstown. We had wondered how the local paramilitaries would respond to this, but one of their leaders was so impressed by the band that he invited us to come back any time we wanted!

That night, after stripping down the sound system and lighting, I tried to get a taxi from Andersonstown to Janice's parents' home in Protestant East Belfast. At that time there had been a spate of sectarian killings where taxi drivers had been lured to hostile parts of the city where gunmen were waiting to kill them. Initially my driver refused to take me where I wanted to go, as he was convinced that I was setting up his assassination. I finally made it to bed in the early hours of the morning. I was so exhausted that I couldn't see how I would be able to drag myself out of bed the next morning to preach. Then I remembered that this was the night that the clocks changed. The clocks were going back, so I had an extra hour in bed! I doubt if a grown man has ever been so glad to see the clocks change. That extra hour of sleep seemed like manna from heaven.

John Grey saw that we were struggling and were looking for some godly spiritual authority, so he suggested we speak to someone from the Church of God. He arranged for their Superintendent over Western Europe, Doug LeRoy, to come and visit us.

The Church of God is the oldest Pentecostal denomination in the world, originating in a revival in the mountains of North Carolina at the end of the Nineteenth Century. Its work in England was pioneered by Jamaican immigrants, and consequently the New Testament Church of God is the largest black denomination in Britain. Because our only contact with the Church of God was through John and his musicians, we thought everybody in the Church of God was black. In fact, we thought we would be the first white Church of God members! So I drove to Belfast airport to meet Doug LeRoy from his flight, fully expecting him to be black. After all, the only people I had ever met who were called LeRoy were all black.

Doug LeRoy is a southern gentleman, and most definitely white. In the end Doug and I were the only people left standing in the Arrivals Hall. He didn't look like my idea of someone called LeRoy, and with my leather jacket and pony tail I probably didn't look like his idea of a Pastor. He came up and asked, "Has the person meeting you not turned up either?" I replied, "No, I'm looking for some black guy named LeRoy!"

Doug spent a few days with us, and I quickly came to respect him as a man of God. I had met plenty of high-flying preachers in my time, but when you got up close you often found that their personal lives didn't match up to their public persona. Some of them would walk straight over you if you stood between them and their ambitions. We weren't looking for flashy superstar preachers. We were looking for integrity. I said to Janice, "If everybody in the Church of God is like Doug LeRoy, then I want to be a part of it."

Since then I've found that not everybody in the Church of God is like Doug LeRoy, but I am so grateful that we found this group of people that provided a spiritual home for us. They have encouraged us, supported us, believed in us, and have invested into the Kingdom of God in Ireland. When Doug was visiting us in Ireland, I thought the main issue was whether we would decide to join the Church or not. Looking back, I think the issue was more whether Doug would accept us into the Church or not. We had three small Churches, were obviously chaotic and overstretched, and I'm sure my long hair and ponytail didn't make me look like a potential Church of God preacher! I'm not sure what it was that Doug Leroy saw in me, but I will be eternally grateful that he believed in us and extended the hand of fellowship.

In September 1995 Janice and I made two important steps. We moved across the border and left Northern Ireland behind in order to be nearer the Church in Drogheda. We also officially inaugurated the Church of God in Ireland, with a grand total of three Churches and thirty-nine members.

13

TOUCHING THE NATIONS

As I look back years later, I see Grace's death and our affiliation with the Church of God as being the key turning points in our ministry in Ireland. Things were still hard work, but that's always how it is with Church planting. If anyone has the notion that you can start something new for God quite easily, then they are kidding themselves. Planting a new Church takes prayer, anointing, and a host of other spiritual things, but it also requires a lot of hard work. I class these events as turning points because previously we had been hanging on by our fingernails, never quite knowing if we were going to make it or not. But now we felt as if the Devil had taken his worst shot at us, and we were still standing. We were here for the long haul, no matter what happened.

Furthermore, Janice was now fully involved in the ministry, sharing the burdens and the joys of the work with me. I often see Church websites where the Pastor's wife is listed as a Pastor herself, even where she does little or no ministry in the Church. Janice is an ordained minister and Pastor in her own right, and I thank God daily for giving me such an awesome woman of God as a friend, as a lover, and as a partner in ministry.

Finances were still unbelievably tight. I remember one Sunday morning where we had no food in the kitchen at all. Janice, Kirsty and I got up early that morning and went through the streets picking up empty beer cans left over from Saturday night. Eventually we figured we had collected enough to sell for their scrap aluminium value, ensuring there would be food in the house for the next few days. I felt an abject failure as I watched my wife and six year old daughter having to scavenge on the streets. What kind of husband and father was I? Later that morning I stood up in front of a tiny congregation and preached, declaring that if we tithe God will open the windows of heaven and pour out a blessing so great that we cannot contain it (Malachi 3:10). All the time I was hoping that nobody would interrupt and ask, "How come it isn't working for you?"

After I had paid all the expenses involved with bringing John Grey and the black Gospel group to Ireland, I was praying for God to somehow miraculously meet our needs. Things were so bad that I was afraid to answer the telephone in case it was the bank manager! Then, totally unexpected, a large cheque arrived from the British government. It was in connection with a welfare payment due to disabled children. We had notified them of Grace's death, but they had made an error and, thinking she was still alive, sent us a lump sum to cover all the weeks that had occurred since then.

I sat and gazed at the cheque. Here was enough money to pay all our bills and to give us some breathing space. I have to admit it was tempting. After all, it wasn't as if we had made any dishonest claims. They had sent us the money without us even asking for it! But in the end there was no doubt as to what we had to do. I wrote a letter explaining that Grace had died, and so we were not entitled to this payment. Then I took the letter to the post office and mailed it.

I've heard people share testimonies about this kind of thing, and how they felt such a release and a freedom afterwards. I didn't feel any release or freedom. I felt sick. I thought to myself, "What on earth have I done? I had the money in my hands to solve our problems, and I sent it back!" Yet something was broken spiritually that day. Over the next week it seemed as if Janice and I had turned into money magnets. Financial blessing flowed in from all kinds of unexpected sources. By the end of the week, the total financial income that came into our household had far exceeded the amount on the cheque that we had returned.

From the first day we commenced this ministry, it seems as if there has never been a time when we have not been stretching our faith and having to believe God for some kind of bill or commitment to be paid. But it has been a source of constant amazement to us how God has provided in remarkable ways.

On one occasion we needed nine hundred and twenty two euro by Monday morning. A payment was due at the bank, so all the preceding week I was praying and believing. Sunday came, but still no sign of the provision we needed to pay the bill. That Sunday we had a guest speaker from South Africa. In fact this was his second time of speaking at our Church in Drogheda. He had visited a year earlier, but I had not been present as I was out of the country.

He began his sermon by turning to me and apologising. He said, "I don't normally do this kind of thing, but God has really laid this on my heart." Then he proceeded to explain to the congregation that God had shown him that their Pastor had a particular financial need, and so they would receive a special offering to bless me. I was stunned. Guest speakers aren't supposed to do this kind of thing – but it was so timely that I couldn't deny that God was at work. The special offering that day amounted to one thousand and twenty five euro. Of course we paid our tithe out of that, which rounded up to one hundred and three euro, which left us with exactly the required sum of nine hundred and twenty two euro to pay into the bank on Monday morning!

That was remarkable enough in itself, but what our guest speaker said next just about blew my mind. He commented, almost as an aside, "Actually God spoke to me about this over a year ago, but when I got here I found your Pastor wasn't here. So I had to wait until this second trip to be obedient." God had known more than a year earlier that we would have this need, and so He had set things in process that, more than twelve months later, would provide the precise sum we needed! Immediately I thought of the Scripture, "Your Father knows what you need before you ask Him." (Matthew 6:8)

When we had left England for Ireland, it seemed as if we were giving up on our dream to touch the nations. But God had other ideas. Someone gave us enough money for me to make an overseas trip. Everybody expected that I would go to the United States. After all, that's where the money is, so it seemed to make sense to go Stateside and raise some much needed financial support. Instead I bought a ticket to Ghana, in West Africa. My reasoning was that we needed prayer even more than we needed financial support. The money might be in America, but African believers know how to pray!

That African trip was a milestone in so many ways. Thousands of African believers committed to pray daily for our churches in Ireland. Not only that, but I caught a fresh vision of a move of God from Ireland that would touch the nations of the earth. There was a time in Ireland's history when it was the primary missionary sending nation in the world! That was back in the Dark Ages when the Celtic Church sent out missionaries to re-evangelise Europe, after so many Christian communities had been wiped out by the Vikings. In Africa I began to understand that God's redemptive gifts for a people might lie dormant, but they never disappear entirely. Ireland could be that missionary nation once again.

In Ghana I also experienced a truly dramatic personal work of healing. Through drinking dirty water, I fell sick with rice-water cholera. I truly thought I was going to die – but the believers there prayed for me, and I was instantly and completely healed.

My next step to touching the nations involved Eastern Europe. Jorge Giron, originally from Guatemala, was serving at that time as the Church of God's Education Director in the former Soviet Union. He asked me to join him on a trip to the Ukraine. I agreed, not realising at the time that it would involve me flying out on our wedding anniversary. Of course, to make matters worse, this would also be the third anniversary of Grace's death. Sometimes I demonstrate such little sense that it is a source of amazement to me that Janice has never tried to divorce me!

The arrangement was that I would catch a flight from London to Vienna, Jorge would fly to Vienna from Stuttgart, and then we would be on the same flight to Odessa in the Ukraine. Jorge assured me that he had arranged that we would sit together on that flight, so he could brief me about all the practical arrangements waiting for us once we got to the Ukraine. Everything went well until I got to Vienna. As I boarded the flight to Odessa, I found my seat and waited patiently for Jorge. Time passed, and then somebody else sat in the seat next to me. The flight attendants closed the doors and we departed. No sign of Jorge! Unbeknown to me, his flight from Stuttgart was delayed, and so he missed the connection. I was on a plane to a strange country, not knowing a word of the language, and I hadn't a clue if anyone would be waiting for me when I got there.

I was feeling a bit apprehensive about Jorge's no-show, guilty at travelling when my place was probably at home with my wife, and was trying not to think too much about it being the anniversary of Grace's death. Janice had gone through a painful, but ultimately healthy, grieving process. But I had never really allowed myself to grieve properly, and was still suppressing my feelings. I decided to distract myself by concentrating on the inflight video.

Austrian Airlines had obviously decided, given the mix of nationalities on this flight, that it would make more sense to show videos that had no dialogue, therefore there would be no need for translation. The first presentation was a Mr. Bean comedy. Then they began to show short Donald Duck movies. I realised that these were the same movies that Grace had loved so much. We had almost worn the VCR out, playing and replaying the same cartoons while Grace roared with laughter every time that Donald had an accident.

To my horror, all the grief I had been suppressing for three years began to come to the surface. I could feel tears coming to my eyes. "Oh God," I silently prayed, "Please don't let me start crying in public while watching a Donald Duck cartoon!" Too late! Now the tears were flowing freely, and soon I was trying to stifle huge audible sobs. The man sitting beside me, in what should have been Jorge's seat, leaned over and whispered in my ear, "Don't worry. It's not real – it's only a cartoon."

So I arrived in Odessa, after the most humiliating flight I have ever experienced. I collected my luggage and walked out into the Arrivals Area. Everyone was shouting at each other in foreign languages, and even the words on the signs seemed to contain letters that were back to front. For about thirty minutes I wandered round the airport, pulling my suitcase after me, but I couldn't see anyone who looked like they were Church of God preachers.

Finally I had a brainwave. I got a piece of paper and drew a cross on it. Then I walked through the airport again, holding this scrawled cross above my head. Two rough-looking guys wearing leather jackets looked up at the sign, started talking to me in Russian, and then motioned to me to follow them. I said, "Church of God?" but they didn't answer me. I followed them to the parking lot, and they pointed at a black car with tinted windows. So I got into the back of the car, and we drove off.

For the next two hours I sat in the back of that car, staring at the back of their heads. What on earth was going on? Who were these men? Where were they taking me? I had heard stories about the Russian mafia, and I was wondering whether it was a smart move to get into a car with strangers based on the fact that I had drawn a cross on a piece of paper.

As we got further away from the airport, the roads seemed to get worse. Finally we turned up a dirt track and stopped outside what looked like a deserted farmhouse. The driver opened my door and motioned to me to get out. He walked in front of me while his companion walked behind me. I felt like I was a dead man walking. The driver led me into the farmhouse.

Inside it was warm, welcoming, and I could see bread, cheese and slices of salami laid out on a table. A big woman smiled at me and said, "Brother Nick, Jorge asked me to tell you that he missed his flight. These brothers who collected you at the airport speak no English, but after supper they will take you to the Church." The next day, when Jorge finally managed to join me, I didn't know whether to kiss him or kill him!

That trip changed the way I looked at World Missions for ever. Up to that point, if you had pressed me, I guess I would have described missionaries as people who travel to other countries to preach salvation to them. I had this mental image of a Billy Graham-type figure standing in a stadium, preaching the Gospel to grateful natives, and then streams of people coming forward in response to an altar call. And that, of course, is what people in the West want to hear about. If you've given your hard earned money to help send a missionary overseas, then you want to hear how many people have got saved as a result. That's what our Church in Drogheda wanted to hear. They would measure my trip to the Ukraine as successful or not based on how many people I could report as having got saved.

I discovered, however, that the Pastors and leaders in the Ukraine were perfectly capable of getting people saved themselves. In fact, judging by the size of their Churches, they were a lot better at that than I was! What they wanted was teaching. They wanted to gain the knowledge and the skills necessary to take their Churches to the next levels of growth, and they were continually asking me questions about this. It was amazing that they should be addressing those questions to me, but what was even more amazing was that I had the answers to those questions.

It took me several trips to the former Soviet Union before I stopped feeling guilty about this. I soon explained to our Church at home that the real need in Eastern Europe was not for evangelists from the West, but rather teachers to equip the local people to evangelise. And, considering my Master's degree studies had majored in Church Growth, I was academically qualified to bring such teaching. But I still felt like a fraud, given that many of my Ukrainian and Russian students already pastored Churches much bigger than mine.

God finally helped me to understand this better by reminding me of a golf coach. Even the greatest golfers still need a coach. Now, if Tiger Woods and his coach were to play a round of golf, who would you expect to win? The answer, of course, is that Tiger would win. If the coach was capable of beating Tiger over eighteen holes, then he would be the one winning the majors and earning multiple millions. But the coach's value does not consist in his ability to beat his pupil. The coach's value is that his input can help Tiger to play even better golf than would otherwise be the case. My value in touching the nations did not depend upon the size of our Churches in Ireland. My value depended on me teaching the principles to my precious Ukrainian brothers that would help them be even more fruitful in their efforts to reach their nation with the Gospel of Christ.

Sometimes God's plan for our lives can be a bit like putting together a jigsaw puzzle without looking at the picture on the box. You have all these pieces, but you can't quite see how they all fit together. Some of them are blue, some of them are mainly green, while others seem to contain little fragments of houses and cars. So you put all the blue pieces at the top, and start to fit them together to form an image of the sky. The mainly green pieces join together to form grass and trees. The fragments of houses and cars gradually combine to give a fuller picture. But for quite a while it seems as if you're completing three or four different jigsaw puzzles. You can't see how the sky, the trees or the other items all relate to each other. Then you have that 'Aha!' moment when it all starts to make sense.

The Church in Drogheda and the other Irish Church plants were starting to fit together well. Now, after visiting the Ukraine, the whole idea of travelling the world to touch the nations was also making sense. But it was hard to see how they could relate to each other. Already I had some people in Drogheda who would say to me, "We don't want to hear your stories of what God is doing in Eastern Europe. We care about what God is going to do here, and we want our Pastor to be here teaching us, not travelling all over the world!" It seemed like these two visions, both of which stirred my passion and felt like they came from God's heart, could detract from each other.

Then, as if that wasn't enough, God threw another part of the puzzle into the mix. I had, at long last, started visiting the United States. On my first two trips I couldn't even rent a car as I didn't own a credit card. I had to travel everywhere on Greyhound Buses. By the time Janice and Kirsty were able to accompany me on a trip to Churches in Florida, we were in a position to rent a car. We arrived into Miami just as a hurricane blew into town. Neither of us had seen anything like it. We were due to arrive the next day at the Cooper City Church of God in Fort Lauderdale, and I had said, "We'll have no trouble finding a hotel for the first night." As it was we spent hours driving round in circles in some of Miami's scariest districts in appalling weather. None of the motels looked at all appealing.

Eventually we were so desperate that I said, "We'll have to stop and check in for the night at the next motel that we see."

The motel proved to be surprisingly cheap, so I handed over my twenty-five dollars and we went to our room. Janice was decidedly unimpressed. The room was filthy. The bedclothes didn't even seem to be clean, and the power kept cutting out. Janice looked up at me with tears in her eyes, "I don't like it here," she said, "I wish we were back home."

We tried to make the best of a bad job. We lay down on top of the bed and tried to get some sleep. Even though the storm continued to howl outside, we were so exhausted by our long flight that we finally dozed off. It only seemed a short time later that we were wakened by someone banging on the door of our room. I staggered to the door, wiping the sleep from my eyes, and saw the receptionist of the motel standing before me. It was still dark outside. "Quick," he shouted, "Time to go!"

I stared at him. Was Miami being evacuated because of the hurricane? Why on earth was he telling us to vacate a motel room in the middle of the night? "Time to go!" he repeated, "Your two and a half hours are up."

"What are you talking about?" I protested, "Two and a half hours? Why on earth would anyone rent a motel room for two and a half hours? What kind of idiot ..... ?" And then I stopped. What kind of idiot would book a hotel room for two and a half hours? Probably an Irish idiot who neglected to book his hotel in advance, and then couldn't tell the difference between a legitimate hotel and a den of prostitution! We were so tired that I paid him another twenty-five dollars to leave us alone until morning, and then went back to bed. Looking back it sounds funny, but what was genuinely sinister was that the motel receptionist had seen that we had a young child with us, yet he was still happy to rent us a room for what he imagined to be immoral purposes.

The next morning we got out of there as quickly as possible. In daylight, and without a hurricane, both the motel and the neighbourhood looked even worse than they had the night before. I looked at Janice as we drove away, winked, and said, "Welcome to America." Thank goodness that Pastor Dwight Allen and the good people of the Cooper City Church treated us wonderfully after that, but when I told them about our experience of the previous night they said, "So *that's* the kind of hotel the Overseer of Ireland likes to stay in!" To this day, every time I visit the Cooper City Church, someone will still remind me about that motel.

Yet God still spoke to us in a powerful way on that visit. The Cooper City Church of God is composed of worshippers from scores of nations. I watched how Pastor Allen cared for a harmonious Church of so many races and nationalities, and it seemed to me that it was like a picture of heaven. So this was another way of touching the nations? Sometimes you can go to the nations, but at other times the nations can come to you. Then God began to sow another vision into my heart, one that was breathtaking in its audacity. Our Church in Drogheda could become a multicultural Church like Cooper City!

But how could that be? Pastor Allen's Church was in the United States, where for centuries immigrants had arrived seeking freedom and prosperity – the tired, the poor, the huddled masses yearning to breathe free. Our Church was in Ireland, a nation where people emigrated elsewhere to find work. How could a Church be multicultural in a country where there only lived people of one culture? How could there be anything like the

Cooper City Church in a place like Drogheda, where ethnic minorities were so rare that black visitors couldn't even walk to a burger joint without becoming objects of curiosity? It seemed like an impossible dream.

Nick Park

14

BECOMING INTENTIONALLY MULTICULTURAL

As the year 1999 was drawing to a close, I became increasingly disturbed by the near hysteria among many Christians about the Y2K Bug. The theory was that computers could not cope with the date change at the new millennium, and that worldwide chaos would ensue. Supposedly planes would fall out of the sky, trillions of dollars would disappear from bank records, cities would be left without power or water, and civilisation would fall apart. In the event, the year 2000 would roll in without a hitch, but sadly Christians were in the forefront of scare-mongering and propagating the Y2K hoax. Some believers were even stockpiling food and making plans to hideout in the mountains!

Now, I am not a computer engineer, so I was in no way qualified to judge how ready computer systems across the globe were for the new millennium. But the problem with the whole Y2K hoax, like so many other stories that Christians gullibly forward in emails, was that it was all based on fear rather than faith. God has not given us a spirit of fear! (2 Timothy 1:7)

In the Solid Rock Church in Drogheda, we began to pray in late 1999. We asked God to fill us with excitement at what He intended to do. We didn't want to swallow a message of fear and gloom. We wanted to enter 2000 in a place of faith and trust. I began to understand that now was the time for us to get ready for being multicultural. So, on the final Sunday of 1999, I made this statement while I was preaching, "In this coming year, 2000 AD, God is going to bring the nations of the world to Drogheda, to this Church, to enable us to touch the nations." That wasn't just wishful thinking – I knew I had heard from God.

So, throughout the year 2000, I kept telling the Church to get ready to receive the nations. I taught on what this might involve. How we might have to adapt the way we programme our services, how we should be proactive in inviting people of other cultures into our homes, how we would need to involve those of other cultures in ministry positions and in leadership.

Week after week of that year went by, but there were no signs of any nations coming near our Church. I kept saying, "Get ready to welcome those of other cultures" – but people were starting to get restless. By the time we got to October I was thinking of how false prophets were stoned in the Old Testament, and wishing that maybe I hadn't been so definite that the arrival of the nations was going to happen this year. Immigrants from other countries were arriving into other parts of Ireland then, but not in Drogheda.

Then, on the last Sunday in November, Tunde and Bisola Oki, from Nigeria, walked into the Solid Rock Church during our morning worship. Since all of our people had been preparing for this moment for the best part of a year, Tunde and Bisola probably received the warmest welcome that any visitor to an Irish Church has ever received! They knew right away that they had found their spiritual home, and their arrival seemed to open the floodgates. Within weeks dozens of immigrants from various nations were worshipping with us. Some of them didn't even speak our language. One Moldovan lady came every week, even though she spoke no English. One Sunday I realised that we had another Russian speaker who could translate, so I asked this Moldovan lady why she came to a Church where she couldn't understand a word that was being said. She replied, "I feel Jesus here."

It turned out that Tunde and Bisola weren't even supposed to be in Drogheda. On arriving in Ireland they had been housed in a Government-run centre in Dublin. They were due to be transferred to Cork, but heavy rains flooded the roads, so they unexpectedly ended up in Drogheda. Being committed Christians they wanted to find a place of worship, so they asked around to find if there were any Pentecostal Churches in town. Someone told them, "I haven't any idea what a Pentecostal is, but there's a crazy group of Christians who meet in a hotel, play loud music, and raise their hands in the air." Pastors Tunde and Bisola Oki served on our Pastoral Team for many years, and now lead Solid Rock Southside, a vibrant new Church plant in Drogheda.

I meet many Pastors who say they want their Church to become multicultural, but what they really want is a multi-coloured audience while they and their fellow leaders continue to do business as usual. That will not cut it. I remember how awkward I felt as a new arrival trying to break into the culture of the Salvation Army – and yet they were from the same city and country as me! So imagine how it feels to walk into a Church with a completely alien culture. We realised that visitors need to see people 'up front' in Church with whom they can identify.

At that time we had a policy in the Church that new members had to wait six months before they could be involved in the worship team or in any kind of up front ministry. That made sense at the time, because we wanted to make sure that people were on board with the vision of the Church. But the sudden influx of visitors represented a window of opportunity that might not be there in six months' time. Therefore we waived that policy in order to ensure that those on the platform would be as multicultural as those in the body of the congregation.

Being multicultural doesn't just happen. You have to be intentional about it. The Solid Rock Church is not just a Church attended by different nationalities. Our Pastoral Team is multicultural. We have a number of worship teams that lead worship, but all of them are multicultural. We also try to identify the needs of different cultural groups so as to share the Gospel with them more effectively.

That was why, on that Sunday in 2001 when Pat O'Boyle held that African/Irish baby, we were dedicating twenty-seven babies. Up to that point, our baby dedications had been fairly quiet affairs. Each time an Irish family had a baby, we would pray over them in Church, a few family members might attend, and then the family might go for a quiet lunch afterwards. But that's not how things work in most parts of Africa. Baby dedications are a community event, where everybody parties, offers congratulations to the family, and dances for the rest of the evening. Most of our new mothers were living in an asylum seekers' centre and had no opportunity to host guests, so we did all that at Church. Such celebrations, complete with African food such as pounded yam and jollof rice, were something entirely new in Ireland. As a result, the local newspapers came and took lots of photographs, and then the resulting publicity attracted more visitors to the Church.

Sometimes meeting people's needs can lead to the most unexpected forms of evangelism. I prayed for one husband and wife who, unbeknown to me, were desperate to have a baby. As I prayed I felt led of the Lord to speak a prophetic word over them. I said, "You've been asking God for something, but it hasn't happened yet. God doesn't want you to give up. He's telling you to keep on trying."

A few months later the wife, obviously pregnant, came to me and said, "We did what you said. We went home that very afternoon and kept on trying. Now look what's happened!" I was thinking that wasn't quite what I had meant, but word of what had happened leaked out. Soon it seemed as if after every service there were lines of women requesting prayer. Each one of them was asking the same thing, "Pray for the fruit of the womb!" Somehow I had become known as the Pastor who prayed for women to get pregnant. But new families kept coming to the Church as a result, and women kept getting blessed with 'the fruit of the womb!'

One day I happened to read in a national newspaper that Ireland was experiencing a shortage of trained nurses in our hospitals. Therefore the health authorities were recruiting nurses in the Philippines. This sounded like opportunity knocking. I contacted a Filipino congregation working with expatriate workers in the Middle East, and they agreed to send a missionary to Ireland. Other Pastors told me quite bluntly that I was stupid. What need could there possibly be for a Filipino missionary in Ireland? As Forrest Gump said, "Stupid is, as stupid does." In the Summer of 2011, I had the joy of preaching at the tenth anniversary celebrations of the Lord of the Harvest Filipino Church of God in Dublin.

Sometimes I have to pinch myself to remind myself that I'm still in Ireland. I needed to find someone to translate for me when I went to preach at our first Brazilian Church of God in Ireland. Then I remembered that we had an Angolan lady in the Drogheda Church. I phoned her and asked, "Katrina, you guys speak Portuguese in Angola, don't you?" So I ended up preaching to a Brazilian congregation, through an Angolan interpreter, in a borrowed Presbyterian Church premises in County Kildare.

On another occasion I preached to a house full of Slovakian gypsies, but the only one of them that could understand any language other than Slovakian was a girl who spoke Portuguese. So I preached in English, one of our Brazilian members translated into Portuguese, and then this girl translated from Portuguese to Slovakian. It took us a while, but we got the message across in the end!

Pastor Emmanuel Might, with his wife Evelyn, hails from Cameroon in West Africa. Today they lead the Solid Rock Church in Dublin – a daughter Church that has turned out to be every bit as multicultural as the mother Church in Drogheda.

God sent us some wonderful workers from all over the world to come as missionaries to minister to Irish people and immigrants alike. Tim Clark was an Oxford graduate, married to a Texan girl called Trena. Jim Sullivan was a crazy cowboy from Pecos, West Texas, who came with his family. Alex Abiola was a Nigerian immigrant to the US, who married Leah in Florida and then brought her to Ireland. And our latest missionaries are Daniel and Millie Sylverston, of Indian ethnicity, born in South Africa, and who came to Ireland after spending many years pastoring in Cleveland, Tennessee! Even our missionaries are multicultural.

We continued with a twin approach of reaching the nations by welcoming immigrants, but also by going on missions trips. Teams from our Churches in Ireland have travelled to share the Gospel in Ghana, in Nigeria, in Cameroon, in the Ukraine, in Russia, in the Czech Republic, in Bulgaria and in China. I have had the privilege of preaching and teaching in Latin America, in many African countries, in most of Europe, in Turkey, in the Middle East, and in Asia. Yet each week our Churches in Ireland also minister in eight different languages.

For me personally, one of the most moving and significant aspects of touching the nations cannot be shared in this book. I have been immeasurably blessed in having the opportunity to minister in 'closed' countries where persecuted Christians risk arrest, torture and even death. As this is an ongoing ministry it would be dangerous for me to divulge any details or to share my stories of ministering to the most inspiring Christians on earth. I would not want to draw the attention of the authorities to my friends there, and neither do I want to say anything that would prevent me from being able to make return visits. One day those stories will be told, either because the oppressive regimes will fall, or because I will be banned from returning and so may write more openly.

In the previous chapter, I compared the unfolding purposes of God for us to a jigsaw puzzle, where apparently unrelated pieces of the puzzle suddenly slot together and make sense. This has happened to us as regards touching the nations. Recently we had a beautiful example of the interaction between welcoming the nations and going to the nations.

One of our Pastors at the Solid Rock Church in Drogheda, Yemi Olorunniwo, put me in touch with Harrison Akinsulie, a

Nigerian minister who leads an outreach to the Tiv and Idoma tribes in the Middle Belt of Nigeria. This is where the Muslim North meets the Christian South, and the battle is on for the hearts and souls of animist villages. Our believers in Ireland have sponsored the digging of wells in places where previously women had to walk miles to fetch drinking water. We were also able to connect Pastor Harrison with believers in the United States who have sponsored the purchase of a fish farm to help the ministry there to become financially self-sufficient. A multicultural medical team has travelled from Drogheda to conduct medical missions in the Middle Belt villages. We praise God that in 2011 forty new Churches from among the Tiv and Idoma people applied to join the Church of God in Nigeria.

Becoming multicultural has definitely taught us that touching the nations is a two way process.

15

FRESH VISION FOR FRESH CHALLENGES

Large and sudden growth is what many Pastors long for. We shout out in our prayer meetings for God to send revival. In reality such sudden growth can bring a huge amount of problems. You cannot lead and administer a large Church in the same way you do a small Church. If growth is steady over a period of time, then you can evolve new structures for the Church. But when growth is sudden, you are so busy dealing with the urgent that it becomes hard to do what is truly important.

It soon became impossible for the Solid Rock Church to continue meeting in a rented hotel ballroom. We discovered we had outgrown every public facility in our town. There was no building available for rent that was large enough to accommodate the Church. Ireland's booming economy was great news in that virtually all our Church members now had jobs, and the wave of immigration provided fertile fields for evangelism. But when property costs over one million euro per acre ($1.3 million in US money), then the boom doesn't seem to be such a blessing.

We eventually purchased two acres of land with some warehouse buildings on the North side of Drogheda. It took a financial step of faith, and wonderful support from the Church of God. Youth groups all over North America washed cars, held dinners, and raised money in all kinds of innovative ways to help us get our own property. Many of our own people worked night

155

and day removing interior walls to form one large worship area out of several warehouse units.

During this construction work, I wondered at one point whether we could pay for everything. A major donation we had been expecting failed to materialise. Then a contractor offered to save us money by evading some Government taxes. I had to laugh at how Satan always produces such temptations at the time when the pressure is the hardest. I explained to the contractor that, as a Church, if we forfeit the blessing and favour of God, then we have nothing. We had to do things honestly.

The leaders of the Church began to fast and pray. Three days later a man walked into my office. He had not heard that we were under pressure, and he wasn't even a member of our Church, but he had just sold a property and he felt God leading him to tithe to the Solid Rock on the sale. The cheque he handed me, for €50,000, was sufficient for us to finish the work and open the building for worship.

Some years ago, on a visit to Moscow, I was talking with Rick Renner. Rick has a unique ministry where he preaches in English, through a Russian translator, and expounds on the significance of Greek words. It sounds crazy, but it works powerfully. After establishing a strong Church in Latvia, Rick moved to Moscow to start a new Church there. Suddenly, quite out of context in our conversation, I said to him, "God's anointing is cumulative, not consecutive." Rick looked at me sharply and asked me to repeat what I'd just said. Then he said, "I'm receiving that."

I strongly believe that was a word from the Lord. In Rick's case it meant that planting another Church was not to be consecutive – a case of going through all the same stuff again.

Instead it was to be cumulative, building on the triumphs, and even the painful lessons, of last time. Faith is like that. You trust God to do one thing, and then you find you have more faith to believe for the next thing. After we had exercised faith to see the Church building open in Drogheda, we found that we had to exercise faith in a very different area, that of our home.

When Janice agreed to marry me, she knew that our life was going to be unconventional. Following God together has been a glorious adventure, but it has often been challenging. Like any wife and mother, Janice longed for her own home, but every time that looked close to happening, it seemed as if God would open up a new ministry opportunity. Any resources we had saved towards a house always seemed to end up being spent on missions projects and outreaches. People have been incredibly kind to us along the way, often helping us pay rent and even providing homes rent-free, but Janice still prayed for a place we could call our own.

One night, during a powerful prayer meeting, God spoke through a word of prophecy and gave her the Scripture that says, "Put your outdoor work in order and get your fields ready; after that, build your house." (Proverbs 24:27) The meaning was clear. We were to concentrate on winning souls in the harvest field, and God would look after the house for which we longed. We felt a total peace that God would provide.

Then, out of the blue, a Christian brother gave us a large gift to help us buy a piece of land. He stipulated that the gift had to be used to assist us in buying or building a home for ourselves. We arranged a mortgage, built the timber frame of the house, and prepared to complete our home. Then, as we were motivating the believers in Drogheda to give sacrificially in a special offering for the new Church building, God spoke to us again. We gave everything we had – everything we were ready to use to complete our home! We were getting the fields ready, but how much longer until we could build our house? We had a half-built home that depressed me every time I looked at it. But we had intercessors in our Church who had more faith in this area than I did! They would regularly drive to the site and pray over our unfinished house.

At this time I was working long hours in ministering to immigrant communities in Dublin. A brother in one of those Churches would greet me every time he saw me. "Brother Nick," he would say, "Are you any closer to building your house yet?" Then, when I told him we had made no more progress, he would say, "I pray for you every day that God will provide for you to complete your house." This would happen nearly every week.

Then, one Sunday, I arrived at that Church and there was no sign of my friend. I missed his greeting, so I asked where he was. "Didn't you hear," I was told, "He won three million euro on the Lottery." I was disappointed that he would play the Lottery, but maybe, just maybe, this could be how God was going to build our home. After all, this was the guy who prayed every day for our house to be completed! But what they told me next quickly shattered that hope. As soon as he collected his three millions, he visited the US embassy, showed them his bank statement, and faster than anyone had dreamed possible he was the latest arrival in the land of the free and the home of the brave. How would our home ever be finished?

Our ministry to the Romanian community in Dublin was a positive example of the Homogeneous Unit Principle that I mentioned in the Introduction to this book. Pentecostalism is strong in Romania, and soon their immigrant Churches in Dublin became the first place Romanians would go to meet others who spoke their language and ate their food. Every week we were seeing new people come to Christ. On one occasion, as I was conducting a wedding, I felt led to conduct an altar call. Fourteen of the guests gave their life to Christ during that wedding ceremony, including the bride's mother. The groom was so excited. He told me that now his mother-in-law was saved, they would never argue. "Trust me," I said, "It doesn't work like that!"

A few weeks later I was conducting another Romanian wedding. At the meal afterwards I had piled my plate high with sarmali – parcels of cabbage leaf stuffed with rice and pork. Another of the Romanian brothers sat down beside me. "Brother Nick," he said, "Some of us have been watching you. You come here week after week, and you don't get paid for it. You teach us, you tell our friends about Jesus, you marry us and dedicate our babies. And we don't even pay you anything to put fuel in your car. We want to do something for you. We want to help you build your house."

I looked around that table, and dozens of young men were nodding their heads in agreement. Then I realised something I had never realised before. They were all working in Ireland's construction boom! There were carpenters, bricklayers, roofers and electricians sitting with me at that wedding meal. The next Saturday I went to look at my half-built house. Workers were swarming all over it like an army of ants! Over the following weeks, those young Romanian Christians provided free skilled labour worth tens of thousands of euro. Not only that, the members of our Church in Drogheda gave freely and sacrificially to purchase materials for the completion of the task.

Every now and again, when we really need a miracle, I walk through our house. I touch the doorframes, the walls, the fireplace and the kitchen units. As I do so, I remember how this all looked so different when the house was half-built. Then I close my eyes and pray, "Lord, You really provided for us back then in a wonderful way. And that's why I know I can put my faith in You right now, and no matter what happens today, I know You'll never let us down." Because faith is not consecutive – it is cumulative.

Every two years the Church of God meets for its General Assembly in the United States. Ministers from all over the world gather to discuss the business of the denomination and to elect leadership for the next two years. The Executive Council, or Council of Eighteen, is elected and empowered to consider and act on all matters concerning the interest and welfare of the Church of God. As the Church of God is an international denomination, with over seven million members around the world, it is important that the nations of the world are represented in leadership. Therefore, at every General Assembly, two members from outside the United States must be elected to the Council of Eighteen.

I was shocked and honoured to be elected in 2008 to serve as one of these international Council members, and then to be re-elected once more in 2010. I had to pinch myself to make sure this was for real. I am not a political person, and I have never striven for that kind of recognition, but it humbled me that a former teenage alcoholic from Belfast could be elected to such a position. That little boy with no mother and a heart full of pain and bitterness, who traced the outlines of countries on a map and dreamed of touching the nations, was chosen to represent the nations by a denomination whose membership is larger than the entire population of Ireland! God must surely have a sense of humour.

If I had written this book two years ago, then this is where the story would end. A dramatic testimony of someone who was despised as a beggar on the streets, eventually gaining the respect of his peers. It's a happy ending, such as we require for all good stories. It has a neatness and a symmetry to it. But in the Kingdom of God, life isn't like that. We don't reach a place of satisfaction and then live happily ever after in a land far away. Instead, like the apostle Paul, we keep pressing on toward the goal to win the prize for which God has called us heavenward in Christ Jesus (Philippians 3:14). And the very phrase 'press on' implies that there are obstacles and challenges that we must press against.

In 2008 the economic difficulties that the United States had been experiencing began to spread across the globe in a contagion of fear and recession. Ireland's overheated property market slumped alarmingly. Foreign investors, primarily French and German Pension Funds, had risked untold billions in loans through Irish banks to property developers. In an act of criminal recklessness and irresponsibility, the Irish Government guaranteed all those investments. The media has reported that the International Monetary Fund and European Union have 'bailed Ireland out.' That is a falsehood. In fact they bailed out those French and German Pension Funds – but the Irish population has been left to pay the bill.

So a tiny country of four million people is now left owing over two trillion US dollars – that's $250,000 for every man woman and child, or a level of debt per head of population that is over five times that of the United States. In order to have any hope of paying this off, our Government surrendered national sovereignty to the International Monetary Fund, which now dictates the country's economic policy. Unemployment has soared, and young Irish men and women are once again emigrating to search for work.

Immigrants are often hit hardest in times of recession, and many of our Churches have over half their membership unemployed, causing tithes and offerings to fall to less than half the levels of two years previously. The Solid Rock Church has been left with huge building payments. So, rather than ending this book by sitting serenely in a place of comfort and prestige, I am rather battling daily with some of the biggest challenges I've ever faced in almost thirty years of Christian ministry and leadership.

From the moment we first united with the Church of God, my goal was for the work in Ireland to become financially self-sufficient and to stand on its own two feet. We wanted to be a missions force rather than a mission field. I was so delighted, by 2008, to have reached the point where we were sending more financial support to others than we were receiving ourselves. Yet today it seems as if we're back to square one. The Solid Rock Church could no longer afford to pay its building payments and also my salary – so I had to go back on the road, visiting Churches in the US to raise support for Ireland once more. I can not begin to describe how frustrating that is for someone who knows their call is to reach the nations.

Economic pressure, however, has the knack of concentrating our minds on what is important. It might sound strange, but I thank God that He has used this economic crisis to deliver an important corrective to our ministry. For years many Pentecostal Christians in other countries, including Ireland, looked to the United States for inspiration. We saw American Churches with buildings and well-staffed facilities that were beyond our wildest dreams. Somehow we got the idea that if we just believed hard enough, worked hard enough and prayed hard enough, then we could have the same kind of Churches in our own countries. Nobody ever stopped to ask if this would be a good thing.

However, during these times of self-examination and reappraisal, I have come to realise that our outlook was fundamentally flawed. Western society is changing. Some people say we are entering a post-Christian age, but that is to misunderstand what is happening. What we are entering should more accurately be termed a *post-Christendom* age. Christianity is about trying to live as disciples of Jesus. Christendom is where the Church holds a dominant position is society and, in many cases, claims special privileges for itself and imposes its values on the rest of society.

It would be very wrong today to describe Europe as post-Christian. In my view there is more biblical Christianity in Europe than we have seen for centuries. But Europe is definitely post-Christendom in that believers are declaring a message that is counter-cultural and rejected by the majority. This requires humility and great courage. The Church has to behave more like the persecuted Church of the first two centuries of Church History, rather than the politically powerful and wealthy institution of later centuries that began to persecute everybody else.

This theme, of how Christianity became Christendom, will be explored in detail in a forthcoming book entitled 'How on Earth Did We End Up Here?' But for now it will suffice to point out that all the available trends and indicators tell us that North American society is heading towards the post-Christendom model as seen in Europe. In other words, European churches are ahead of the curve in this change process. Instead of striving to be like American churches, European churches can demonstrate how it is possible to be fruitful and effective in the post-Christendom landscape that American churches must soon confront.

Of course European and American Christendom are not identical. Our ways of doing church, unless we remain closely anchored in Jesus, tend to ape and mimic the structures of our surrounding society. European Christendom first developed under the Roman Empire, so the church adopted the methods and structures of the Empire. Clergy adopted the rich dress and claims to power of the nobility, and even became known as 'princes of the Church.' So European Christendom acted as if the Church was a powerful royal family.

The United States, of course, is historically a Republic – very sensibly rejecting the concepts of King and Empire. So American Christendom has followed two competing dominant features of US society, Wall Street and Hollywood. The Wall Street model treats the Church as if it were a business. Pastors, depending on the size of their Churches, act like CEO's or middle-management, and Church members are treated as consumers. Success is measured in terms of attracting the maximum amount of consumers and keeping them happy. If a Church doesn't keep its consumers happy, then they find another outlet that will 'meet their needs' or where they 'feel more comfortable.'

In the Hollywood model of Christendom, Pastors are media celebrities. The most successful practitioners have their own TV shows, and a celebrity life style complete with bodyguards, autograph signing, and even the same kind of moral scandals that characterise Hollywood. Church members, in this form of Christendom, are essentially an audience. The bigger the audience you can attract, the louder the applause and the richer the rewards.

Again, these themes will be explored much more thoroughly in a planned future volume, entitled 'Pilgrim Through This Fruitful Land.'

At the Solid Rock Church we had, like most European Pentecostals, emphatically rejected the Royal Family style of European Christendom. If anything, we had gone in the opposite direction as a reaction against the rites and trappings of Catholicism. The Hollywood model, while perhaps tempting to all of us who operate in the public eye, was also rejected. I simply don't have enough of the showman in me to expect anyone to take me seriously as a religious superstar. But, I am ashamed to say, we had started to pursue a wrong course in managing the Church as though it were a business. The harsh realities of a broken national economy threw this into sharp relief and gave us an opportunity to follow a more biblical path.

The Servant model of Church recognises that believers are not called to follow Jesus in order to be entertained or to be happy. As disciples we learn to get out of our comfort zone, lay down our demands and rights, and serve one another in love as disciples. The leaders in such a Church, rather than living like princes or executives, are called to be the most humble servants of all.

To change the course and ethos of a Church, especially one that is perceived from the outside to be healthy and successful, is a nerve-wracking process. One factor in our favour is that multicultural Churches, by their very nature, demand a deeper level of discipleship and commitment from their members. Worshipping alongside those of other races and cultures creates so many opportunities for misunderstanding and friction that you cannot get by on surface level Christianity – you have to seek extra grace.

One of the greatest spiritual developments that is arising in post-Christendom Europe is that of the 24/7 Prayer Movement. Young people from different Churches, including both traditional denominations and radical new Church plants, are uniting together to maintain an unbroken vigil of prayer in their towns and cities. Their spiritual inspiration comes, not from the wealthy and powerful structures of the past, but rather from the despised and persecuted Moravians who so influenced John Wesley three centuries ago. Part of our vision in Ireland is to establish a non-stop 24/7 Prayer Centre, where there is continual prayer, intercession for the nations, and worship to God.

So, as we look to the future, I am immensely excited by what lies ahead. God is doing something incredible and pioneering, even in a situation of national economic meltdown. I look back in wonder at where God has brought me from, and where He has brought me to. He took a man from rock bottom, to touching the nations. But I am still far from finished, not even fifty years old yet. If God has brought me through such an incredible journey over the last thirty years, then I can't even begin to imagine what lies in the future.

Nick Park

SUCCESS SERVICES IRELAND

If you would like to contact Nick, or to find out more about his writings and teaching materials, please visit www.nickpark.ie

We already stock two other titles by Nick Park, with more releases planned in 2014

Faith - the Real Thing (Second Edition). Originally published by SSI in 1999, this Practical Commentary on Hebrews Chapter Eleven outlines life-changing spiritual principles with humour and passion.

Living Life as a Learner. A discipleship course designed to be used in three different ways. Firstly, as individual reading for a new Christian. Secondly, it can be a useful tool for a small group to study. Thirdly, it is designed for one-on-one discipleship.

How on Earth Did We End Up Here? (Summer 2014) A book on Church History that isn't a history book! Instead Nick Park explores how the Church that Jesus established ended up where it is today. We can't even begin to plan direction for the future if we don't understand how we got to where we are now.

Myths, Lies & Howlers From the Fringes of the New Atheism. (Autumn 2014) Young Christians are often attacked and bombarded through online media with a series of urban legends and assaults on Christianity that are poorly researched and, at times, just plain untruthful. This book lays bare some of the more outrageous and popular new atheist myths.